BLUE RIDGE PARKWAY GUIDE

Rockfish Gap to Grandfather Mountain

**Rockfish Gap to
Grandfather Mountain**

0.0 – 291.9 miles

Blue Ridge Parkway Guide

by William G. Lord

Menasha Ridge Press

Menasha Ridge Press
3169 Cahaba Heights Road
Birmingham, AL 35243

Library of Congress Cataloging—in—Publication Data

Lord, William George, 1921 —

    Blue Ridge Parkway Guide : Rockfish Gap to
    Grandfather Mountain 0.0 to 291.9 miles
    by William G. Lord
    p. cm.
    Rev. ed. of: The Blue Ridge Guide. 1959—1963 Includes bibliographical
    references.

    ISBN 0—89732—118—9

    1. Automobile Travel — Blue Ridge Parkway (NC and VA) Guide-
    books.
    2. Blue Ridge Parkway (NC and VA) Guidebooks.

I. Title
GV1024.L584   1992
917.55--dc20   92-28238   CIP

The author thanks the following for their assistance: Superintendent Gary Everhardt, Resident Landscape Architect Bob Hope, Historian Dr. Harley E. Jolley, and Interpreter Hoyt C. Roth, all of the Blue Ridge Parkway; Superintendent J. Moyer, U.S. Postal Service, Charlottesville, Va.; John H. Reeves, Jr., Virginia Military Institute, Lexington, Va.; Virginia State Extension Specialist W. A. McElfresh, Blacksburg, Va.; Hugh Morton, Grandfather Mountain, Linville, N.C.; Prof. Lewis E. Anderson, Department of Botany, Duke University, Durham, N.C.; Alice Carol Tuckwiller, Roanoke Public Library, Roanoke, Va.; Odell Little, Jefferson, N.C.; Office of the Mayor, Galax, Va.; Bea Simpson, Community Action Programs, Galax, Va.; Mary H. Esser, Public Information Specialist, U.S. Forest Service, Asheville, N.C.; and E. F. Striplin, Jr., Norfolk and Western Railway, Roanoke, Va. Special thanks are due Agnes M. Elton, Pittsburgh, Pa. for manuscript preparation and Dr. Cratus Williams, Appalachian State University, Boone, N.C. for review of folk language.

Blue Ridge Parkway

The Blue Ridge Parkway idea probably originated in the mind of a motorist years ago, traveling over a bumpy mountain road. "How nice it would be," he mused aloud, "if there were a smooth, easy way over the mountains and we could lazy-along and enjoy the view."

The idea found a place in the minds of many men, but for years it had to wait. Building a road through the mountains is a giant task.

Now the Parkway is a reality. It happened something like this. On a pleasant summer day in August 1933, President Franklin Delano Roosevelt came to Shenandoah National Park, Va., on an inspection tour of the Civilian Conservation Corps. Among his most enjoyable miles were those viewing scenery on Shenandoah's Skyline Drive.

Virginia's Senator Harry F. Byrd, a member of the presidential party, suggested the grandiloquent project of constructing a road over the mountain crests connecting Shenandoah and Great Smoky Mountains National Parks. President Roosevelt gave his enthusiastic approval and the idea moved toward reality.

The Administration placed the project under the joint authority of the National Park Service and the Bureau of Public Roads. Virginia and North Carolina contributed to the venture by purchasing land for the motor road right-of-way, and on June 30, 1936, the Seventy-fourth Congress passed the act giving legal status to the Blue Ridge Parkway.

When news reached Aunt Caroline Brinegar, a-sittin' and a-rockin' in her cabin high in the Blue Ridge by Air Bellows Gap, she slapped her knee and laughed at such "an onheered of notion. One of them hard surface roads like they have below the mountains? Why, Lord have mercy, no body a-livin' could put one of them through here."

Still, Aunt Caroline was mighty interested. Every Sunday she'd pause from a-trompin' the treadles of her four-poster loom and hurry across the hollow to Mrs. Krause's and have her read the weekly news. The many articles about Parkway plans and progress soon had her believing "they just might build a road."

Then one day she heard dogs a-barkin', and looking out from the porch stoop she saw surveyors with their chains and rods. Then she knew the road was a-comin' fur sure.

The Parkway is a way of travel through the Southern Highlands dedicated to the recreation motorist. In a manner of thinking it expresses the cooperation of the engineer and landscape architect. The engineer solved and smoothed the obstacles of a seemingly impassable terrain. The landscape architect healed the road scars with green and designed parking overlooks and recreation areas for leisurely enjoyment. Log cabin exhibits along the way preserve the tang of old-timey days.

Recreation areas, varying in size from several hundred to several thousand acres, are wilderness gems for those who enjoy the

Stone fence and woodbine

out-of-doors. Development for visitor use includes picnic grounds, camp and trailer sites, rest rooms, water fountains, and hiking trails.

Service stations, lodging, eating facilities, and handicraft shops operated by concessionaires are at intervals along the way. Nearby are varied resort facilities generally indicated by standard Parkway signs.

The Parkway extends 469 miles from its Shenandoah National Park terminus at Rockfish Gap, Va., to the Great Smoky Mountains National Park at Cherokee, North Carolina. Every mile is maintained and protected by the Parkway staff.

Another part of the Parkway team, the agronomist, meets with Parkway neighbors and arranges the leasing of government land that is suitable for pasture and crops. The farm scene is thereby brought to the roadside and the 800-foot strip of Parkway flows along in harmony with the native landscape. The Parkway also extends through long stretches of National Forests, guardians of our timber and water resources.

The park ranger force, manned by men and women in forest green uniforms and broad-brimmed hats, patrols the motor road to serve the Parkway visitor and protect the area.

Park naturalists, by means of exhibits, living history demonstrations, nature trails, and illustrated lectures, interpret the storied highlands and make a visit more meaningful and enjoyable.

Headquarters are in Asheville, N.C. The Blue Ridge Parkway, a unit of the National Park System, welcomes your visit. The Parkway is yours to enjoy and protect.

Mountain Ranges Along the Blue Ridge Parkway
Most of the Parkway's 469 miles roll atop 355 miles of the Blue Ridge. The remaining distance is through the heart of the Southern Highlands over the Black Mountains, the Great Craggies, Pisgah Ledge, and the Great Balsams. The last group intersects still another range, the Plott Balsams, extending on either side of the Parkway like the wings of a great eagle.

The Blue Ridge, stretching from Pennsylvania to Georgia, forms the eastern rampart of the central and southern Appalachians. The Appalachians comprise the great eastern mountain system extending from Canada to Alabama.

The Parkway commences its journey at Rockfish Gap, rolling southwest from Shenandoah National Park. For over a hundred miles en route to Roanoke, Va., the mountains form a massive barrier rising between the piedmont foothills on the east, and the Great Valley on the west. Beyond the valley loom the Alleghenies. Midway to Roanoke the mountains are severed by the seven-mile gorge of the mighty James, flowing from the Alleghenies to the Atlantic. At this point, mile 65, the Parkway dips to its lowest elevation, 650 feet. It soon weaves up to the crest line again, and on Apple Orchard Mountain attains its highest elevation in Virginia, 3,950 feet above the sea.

From Apple Orchard the Parkway gradually descends through a deep green forest of hemlock and hardwoods onto a long finger of the

Blue Ridge pointing into the Roanoke basin. Again the view commands the horizon, east and west. The city of Roanoke, within the basin, lies surrounded by the Blue Ridge and the Alleghenies.

Between miles 102-132, the Parkway cruises below the western slopes of the Blue Ridge, across the Roanoke River Valley. The Roanoke flows leisurely from the nearby Alleghenies through a broad break in the mountain wall. In this vicinity the Blue Ridge is actually a discontinuous series of free-standing elevations.

South of the Roanoke lies the Blue Ridge plateau, a long uplands wedged between the piedmont and the Great Valley. Here the Blue Ridge forms the eastern rim of the plateau—a ridge in name only.

The Parkway travels close by the rim, with a view of rolling mountain farmland and frequent vistas of the misty piedmont. At mile 216.9 the Parkway and the Blue Ridge move into North Carolina, 252 miles from Great Smoky Mountains National Park.

The Carolina portion of the plateau builds up from a rolling uplands to a surging array of humpbacked mountains and swooping valleys. At Ridge Junction, mile 355, the unruly terrain runs into the massive sides of the Black Mountains, while the Blue Ridge swings southeast on its way to Georgia.

The Parkway skirts the southern edge of the short, ponderous Blacks through a virgin forest of spruce and balsam—and into the heartland of the highlands.

From the adjoining Great Craggies, with their weird forest of wind-stunted trees, the Parkway enters the Asheville area and the French Broad River Valley. As in the Roanoke region, the Blue Ridge lies eastward. But here the river finds no passage to the ocean and so flows over the long inland route to the Mississippi.

Pisgah Ledge carries the Parkway from Asheville southwest to Tanasee Bald. Scenery is breathtaking over the entire Parkway, but from Pisgah Ledge it portrays the meaning of spectacular.

From Tanasee Bald the Parkway swings northwest along the Great Balsams. Like the Blacks, they form one of several transverse ranges at right angles to the northeast southwest trend of the Appalachians.

At Richland Balsam, mile 431, the Parkway attains its maximum elevation of 6,053 feet.

En route to the Great Smokies, the Parkway bisects the Plott Balsams and then gradually descends through the land of the Cherokee. Here is journey's end or beginning, whichever way you take it.

The Mountain Men

The first white men in these rugged highlands were hunters and traders, questing pelts from the game-rich wilderness. From their flintlock sojourns of the 1600s, knowledge of the West came to the land-seeking voyagers ever arriving from across the sea.

The English of the coastal region showed little desire to settle the strange mountain country. Hunter tales, undoubtedly spiced with exaggeration, described it as a place of terrors and savages. Actually—though not generally known at the time—the native Indians were being exterminated through the vicious efficiency of Iroquois raiders, whiskey, and smallpox.

Virginia's colonial government, seeking a buffer against the French, encouraged Scotch-Irish migrants arriving at Philadelphia to move onto land behind the Blue Ridge at bargain prices. Few migrants came at a more opportune time. Almost devoid of human life, the Virginia mountains and their fertile valleys lay waiting for men daring enough to possess them.

From 1725 until the coming of the French and Indian War in 1754, they moved southwest from Philadelphia over an old Iroquois war path. Their route extended along the Great Valley, a tremendous trough between the Alleghenies and the Blue Ridge.

At the present site of Roanoke the trail followed by the migrant stream forked. One branch continued along the Great Valley into the Cherokee country of East Tennessee. The other cut east through the Blue Ridge by the Roanoke River and then resumed its southwest direction into the land of the Catawbas near Charlotte, N.C. The latter route was more heavily traveled and became known over its entire length from Philadelphia as the Carolina Road.

The Scotch-Irish came prepared for a fight, whether against the elements, the Indians, or both. Hard times in north Ireland made them grimly resolved to set matters right in America.

Their history as a separate stock began during the reign of James I, king of England from 1603 to 1625, when that "wise fool" confiscated the lands of rebellious nobles in the Ulster section of Ireland. After removing most of the native element, James invited Scotch lowlanders and people from northwest England to settle what is now known as Northern Ireland. For a century they lived reasonably content until their prosperous sea trade prompted the parliament of George I (1714-1727) and George II (1727-1760) to legislate them out of business. These economic body blows, coupled with crop failures, brought hard times upon the people and they began to heed agents enticing colonists to America.

Another large group of settlers came to the mountains from Germany where they had been forced into wretched conditions by the Thirty Years War.

The Scotch-Irish, German, and some English spread southwest, augmented by an English movement directly inland from the coast. By 1754 their outpost settlements approached the Carolina border. Then red vengeance broke upon the frontier as tribes from the northwest spread torch and terror during the dark years of the French and Indian War. Many isolated cabins were destroyed and many settlers fled without a fight. But others stayed on, fought back, and defeated the enemy. A young colonial officer named George Washington learned to face adversity in a manner that gave him the necessary courage at Valley Forge. Without the "tempering" of Washington's steel in the Indian wars, he might never have realized the final victory at Yorktown.

At the peace conference in Europe, the English Crown decreed that colonists be forbidden to take up lands on westward-flowing waters. The obvious purpose was to protect the Indians and a lucrative fur trade. The proclamation affected nearly all the holdings southwest of Roanoke.

Although the established settlers paid little heed to the King's decree, it diminished movement in the mountains in favor of still unsettled areas along the eastern foothills of Virginia and North Carolina. Here, of course, waters drained eastward to the Atlantic.

During the turbulent years before the Revolution the surge of the Scotch-Irish recommenced, pushing into the highlands from Philadelphia and Charleston, S.C. Naturally, there were numerous other routes, and the immigrant train included other nationalities. In general they came from the British Isles and Germany, with an occasional influx of French Huguenots.

As the pre-Revolution tensions began to build, many colonists made for the mountains. At first they were those inclined toward rebellion. In 1771 a group of Carolina "Regulators" fled over the mountains to the Watauga settlement in northeast Tennessee after losing a fight with the Crown at the battle of Alamance. In later years the Tories were the ones seeking a mountain refuge.

During the Revolution conquest of the highlands slackened, but mountain men were sufficiently entrenched to whip the King's men at Kings Mountain, and shortly to destroy the Cherokee power.

Even before the British surrender at Yorktown, the surge into the Carolina highlands recommenced. Prime movers were the veterans of the Indian campaigns, favorably impressed by the rich bottomlands of the Cherokee country. Before the turn of the century, the entire survey along the Parkway from Rockfish Gap to the Smokies became the white man's domain.

Gradually a distinctive pattern of livelihood grew up. High meadows, probably burned clear of forest by the Indians, proved excellent for cattle, sheep, and horses. Dense stands of chestnut and oak provided an autumn fattener for droves of hogs and flocks of turkeys and geese. Each fall great herds of livestock and fowl were gathered from the mountain farms and driven to markets north and east.

In exchange for meat on the hoof the mountaineer got manufactured items his remote highlands could not supply. His was a simple but sufficient way of life and preserved a great degree of self-reliance. Families made their own clothes by spinning wheel and loom; grew, raised, or hunted their food; and built their own homes.

Schools were almost nonexistent. Many original settlers knew how to read and write, but this gradually slipped away from their offspring.

Religion became the great binding force of the region. During the 1820s the entire nation experienced a religious revival, sparked by the Baptists, Methodists, and to a lesser degree, by the Presbyterians. The more dedicated of their ministers braved every travel hardship to bring the gospel to the isolated and eager mountaineer. The roughest weather hindered them not. As an old saying goes,

"Thars nothing about in this weather but crows and Methodist ministers."

The religious way of life perseveres today much in character with the time of its origin, but the general way of life became tragically torn during the Civil War.

The plight of the plantation South has been eulogized in song and story, but the fate of the Southern Highlands is one of our Nation's untold tragedies. Throughout the region conflicting loyalties set family against family, brother against brother. In general the townsfolk sided with the Confederacy while the hill farmers remained true to the Union.

The mountains became a refuge for gangs of deserters and bushwhackers, pillaging the homes of men gone to war.

Recovery came slowly. While the nation began the painful mending process, the mountains became an isolated province, more than ever a land of make-it-yourself-or-do-without. Time, of course, did not stand still. It was just hemmed in.

The principal reason for this enduring isolation was lack of communication. Community efforts, prior to the Civil War, maintained a passable road system, traveled by stage coach and freight wagon. In the demoralized times that followed, most roads became two parallel ruts, difficult in fair weather and impassable in foul. Most people traveled in the saddle or on foot.

For a period in the late 1800s, it appeared that the mountains might become the heart of a vast mining and metal works. Northern and European capital was invested in numerous enterprises based on promising deposits of ores and minerals. But with the exception of North Carolina's Spruce Pine district and its bonanza of mica, feldspar, and kaolin, few such ventures thrived.

In the early 1900s the mountains gave the appearance of one great lumber camp as mountain men turned lumberjacks cut stands of virgin evergreens and hardwoods. Since the creation of national forests in 1916, the mountain timber has become a carefully harvested resource.

With the decline of mining and timbering, the Southern Highlands gradually returned to the agricultural pattern of pre-Civil War days, improved and more productive, but essentially the same in character. A substantial increase in road building, particularly since the 1930s, opened the highlands as never before. The present thriving economy is indebted to that invention behind road building, the automobile.

The last few decades have brought the present to the past. Electricity has replaced the kerosene lamp, which in turn so tardily replaced the pine knot torch. The auto and pickup truck now provide transportation instead of horse and ox. And the conveniences of modern times, television, deep freezes, and clothes dryers, come with every trailer truck roaring up the mountain. In return go loads of cabbage, apples, burley tobacco, livestock, dairy products, and lumber.

These changes have affected the mountaineer more than the mountains. To a degree the mountains are reverting to long, long ago. The plow has given up its struggle with the steep hillsides and once again they are green with forest, orchard, and pasture. The more level lands grow cereals and row crops bounded by miles of rail fence. And the log cabin of old-timey days, though now used primarily as a barn or shed, is a part of many a homestead.

Many old timers throughout the mountains have known yesteryear. Customs of their day and time still endure. Each spring folks tramp the highlands meadows for "sallet greens." Summer is a time happy with family reunions. Fall is busy with hog killin', running the sorghum press, and boiling kettles of apple butter. Any time of year the fiddle, banjo, and guitar team up and set feet a-stompin' in high glee to "Old Joe Clark," "Sourwood Mountain," or "Fisher's Hornpipe." The Southern Highlands is an awakened region with a feeling for the past and an eye on the future.

The Blue Ridge Parkway, a noncommercial way of mountain travel, has pioneered the most recent awakening. From all America, people come to enjoy the scenery and cool summer climate. Charmed and delighted by this rustic form of recreation, they come again, and again, and again.

Names Uncle Newt Calls 'Em

Our Parkway story grew from many sources such as libraries and courthouse records. But much came from a friendly, ever helpful group of mountain folk along the Parkway. These good neighbors are the honorary historians of their community. "You just go see Uncle Newt. He kin tell you 'most anything they is to know about."

From these many conversations Uncle Newt was born, a make-believe yet very real mountain man who "draps in" every few pages with his seasoned brand of mountain lore.

Uncle Newt is neither young nor old; he's just sort of today-like. He has a boy in the Army, and one daughter a-courtin', and two young'uns fur helpin' out about the farm.

The family—wife, man, and offspring—raise their own eggs and meat, do a heap of cannin' from the garden, and make most of their cash crop from burley, cabbages, apples, and sellin' a few Herefords each fall.

Uncle Newt is right proud of his most recent possession, a quarter-ton pickup, so new "hit still don't smell of the barnyard."

To avoid any misunderstanding: many of our local contacts had college degrees, spoke perfect English, and, like Uncle Newt, were gracious and helpful. Uncle Newt was born out of love and admiration for the mountaineer local color he represents.

With Uncle Newt's assistance, we'll endeavor to describe the geographic terms of the Southern Highlands.

Bald A high mountain that has (or had at the time it was named) a treeless area on or near its summit. The treeless patch may be barren or covered with grass or shrubs. Many of these fields are believed to have been caused by fires, repeatedly set by the Indians for game clearings. They are gradually returning to forest, some more rapidly than others, depending on the climate. Craggy Gardens, mile 364.

Bluffs "A big ole mountain that dips off sharp down one side." The Bluffs of Doughton Park, mile 241.

Butt "Ever had someone say he'd like to kick you in the pants? Well this here butt has a callin' likeness." Our map makers tend to change certain of the original names they consider too "salty." Craggy Pinnacle, mile 364.4, was once known as Buckner's Butt.

Cliff "A big ole rocky ridge and plenty steep. Most folks calls'm 'clifts.' " A rare term. Cedar Cliffs of Doughton Park, mile 241.

Dome A round-topped mountain, like a knob, but one of great stature. Craggy Dome, mile 364.1.

Peak A prominent, steep mountain, such as Clingman's Peak, seen at mile 349.9.

Piedmont The foothill country between the Blue Ridge and the Atlantic Coastal Plain.

Pinnacle A sharp, conical mountain. Craggy Pinnacle, seen at mile 364.4.

Range   A group of mountains defined by surrounding lowlands and forming a major drainage divide, or, of sufficient extent and prominence to be classified as a range. The Parkway traverses the following ranges: Blue Ridge, Black Mountains, Great Craggies, Pisgah Ledge, Great Balsams, and the Plott Balsams.

Ridge   The term is variously applied but always refers to "a long, sharp edged mountain. Sometimes a ridge makes up a whole mountain and sometimes hits nothin' more'n a spur." Whetstone Ridge, mile 29.4.

Spur   "A long kind of ridge reachin' away from the mountains like a buzzard's wing." The best illustrations are the narrow, winglike projections tapering down from the eastern edge of the Blue Ridge south of Roanoke, Va. Pine Spur, mile 144.8, and High Piney Spur, seen from Fox Hunter's Paradise, mile 218.6.

Top   A descriptive term typical of the Pisgah and Balsam country.

Bottom   "A bottom's the flat land 'longside of a stream below the mountains."

Cove   There are two kinds of coves. One is a small, straight valley down a mountainside. Cove is also applied to an extensive flatland more or less surrounded by mountains. North Cove, seen from Chestoa View, mile 320.7.

Crest line   An imaginary line dividing an elevation, lengthwise, and forming the drainage divide for streams flowing down either side.

Flats   "A flat kind of place some'rs part way up a mountain. The Norvell Flats was big enough fur the South River Lumber Company to yard thur engines." Norvell Flats, mile 34-35.

Gap   "See the outline of that mountain over thar? Them low dips in it's what's knowed as a gap. Some of 'm is whar a road or trail is located acrost the mountains." In general, the Parkway travels the crest line of the Blue Ridge and several other ranges. Therefore, it passes through a long series of gaps and intersects many cross-mountain roads.

Glade   A grassy, open place in the forest. Sections of the high Balsam Mountains, miles 424-442, are referred to as glades because of the grassy areas beneath the stunted wind-spread trees. Glades were also made by Indians, within and below the mountains, by burning large areas of forest for game clearings.

Hollow   "A little hollered-out place at the foot of a mountain." Iron Mine Hollow, mile 96.5. Hollows formed at the heads of streams, against a mountainside, have long been favorite cabin sites. The land was level enough for a garden and a corn patch, and close by a spring.

> "I'm goin' to set me down at the head of a holler,
>   An' build me a home sweet home,
> I ketched me a woman, a gun, and a dawg,
>   An' I got no cause to roam."

Levels   The levels tell an interesting geological story. These broad mountain summits are believed to be the remnant of an ancient plain uplifted to mountainous heights. Subsequent erosion has dissected much of the levels into ridges and valleys. Big Levels, seen on the left from Greenstone Overlook, mile 8.8.

Meadow   In the early days the term ''meadow'' often applied to grassy clearings, many of which lay like bright green patches on a mountainside. The appropriately named Crabtree Meadows Recreation Area, mile 339.3, was formerly known as Blue Ridge Meadows.

Notch   A rare term for ''gap'' in the Southern Highlands. It is typical of New England, as the term ''pass'' is for the West. Low Notch, mile 239.9.

Pass   As used regionally, pass is a rare term referring to a way between the mountains, usually along a stream. In the West a pass refers to a way across the mountains. Goshen Pass, along the Cowpasture River between Lexington and Goshen, Va.

Saddle   ''Looks jest like it sounds.'' A saddlelike depression between two high points on a crest line. The Saddle, on Rocky Knob, mile 168.

Slicks, Hells   Following a fire, a mountainside with sufficient moisture frequently is covered by an almost impenetrable jungle of rhododendron or mountain laurel. The shiny leaves of the mountain laurel give rise to ''ivy slicks'' on the steep mountainsides. The jungle-like growths may also be known as ''laurel hells,'' or ''ivy hells.'' Following a burn, dry slopes generally re-cover with the black and Table Mountain pines.

Swag   ''That's kindly a long, shaller place along the tops of the mountains.'' Long Swag, mile 433.7.

Valley   A long depression between two parallel highlands. In general, they are named for streams that drain them. The Great Valley extends like a trough through the entire Appalachians from New York to Alabama. It is seen west of the Parkway from miles 0 to 100. Since the Great Valley is drained by several rivers, portions of it have regional or local names. The Shenandoah Valley is that portion drained by the Shenandoah River. A large valley has several inlet valleys, just as a large river has several tributaries. Arnolds Valley, mile 78, leads from the Blue Ridge into the Great Valley.

Branch   ''Ever heard tell of branch water? Nothin' like it. Comes fresh out of a spring and then sort of branches into a bigger waters.''

Fork   ''Lots of mountain streams fork together at the bottom of some mountain. Each one's called a fork.'' Pisgah Ledge country, miles 412-23.

Prong   ''About the same as a fork, but mostly smaller. Prongs mostly feed into forks.'' Pisgah Ledge country, miles 412-23.

Run   ''A small, feeder stream that makes a beeline scoot down the mountain.'' Big Spy Run. Flows below Big Spy Overlook, to the right, mile 26.4.

Watershed   As used regionally, an area in the mountains whose streams fill reservoirs for use by local communities and industries. Asheville Watershed, miles 355-370.

Anywhere along the way you might happen upon Uncle Newt, resting his elbows on a rail fence, smokin' his pipe, and being friendly like.

The Blue Ridge Mountains of Virginia

Rockfish Gap, Va., to Roanoke, Va.
(0.0 to 121.4 miles)

Although the Blue Ridge Mountains extend from southern Pennsylvania to Georgia, they are most representative of their name through northern Virginia. Here they form a great master ridge that dominates parallel lowlands on either side. Eastward are the piedmont foothills. Westward, between the Blue Ridge and the Alleghenies, lies the Great Valley, the route of the pioneers.

From Rockfish Gap south to the James, where the big river has gnawed a seven-mile gorge through the mountains, the Parkway curves along the Blue Ridge crestline. From its low elevation of 650 feet at the James, the Parkway again ascends the crest at elevations approaching 4,000 feet. The mountains gradually decline in height but not in rugged grandeur as they approach Roanoke Valley.

The Roanoke River apparently had no struggle to find a passage through the mountains. By the river they are low and humble. They mark the southern limit of the songwriter's ''In the Blue Ridge Mountains of Virginia.''

South of the Roanoke the Blue Ridge forms the high eastern rim of the Blue Ridge plateau—no longer a master ridge above the bordering lowlands. Terrain between Rockfish Gap and Roanoke is both harsh and serene. We have learned this land serves best as a reservoir of our timber and water, and for scenic enjoyment and recreation.

From the beginning of mankind's adventure, this turbulent terrain has never supported more than a sparse human population. Hunting and warring parties of Shawnee, Delaware, and Iroquois from the north frequently paused and established temporary camps. The native Saponi and Totero also ranged the mountains, but built their villages and planted their cornfields by the large riverbanks. In the early 1700s when white hunters and explorers penetrated the region, they came in contact with bears more often than fellow humans.

By 1730 settlers began to move from Pennsylvania down the Great Valley. A gradually increasing number crossed the mountains from eastern Virginia. Few, however, stayed in the mountains. The valley migrants were newly arrived from Europe, predominantly from north Ireland and the German Rhineland. Settlers who populated the eastern foothills came largely under the leadership of tidewater gentry, moving inland for tobacco and grazing land. Unlike the small freeholders of the valley, they established large plantations and utilized slaves to a much greater extent. A sectional rivalry, generally of the good-natured sort, soon commenced between the two regions. The valley people came to be known as ''Congaree,'' while those on the eastern side referred to themselves as "Tuckahoe." The Blue Ridge barrier between them became the haunt of the footloose hunter, outlaw, runaway slave, and a scattering of homesteaders. Large sections of the mountains were used to run livestock, and portions were enclosed by stone fences to contain herds of razorback hogs.

The Civil War brought the breakup of the large plantations and the transfer of much of their mountain holdings to mining corporations. Although many minerals and ores were found in fair quantity, the hoped-for boom never materialized. Most operations gradually shut down after an off-and-on existence.

In 1912 the federal government began buying up submarginal land to be included in the newly created National Forests, the George Washington north of the James River, and the Thomas Jefferson to the south. Here and there a highland farmer has achieved success and harmony on a stretch of level uplands, and still remains. But most mountain farmers were glad to be relieved of their struggle with the mountains. The forest soon reclaimed the "hanging cornfields" and the steep impossible pastures.

The Parkway rides the watershed divide, high above distant views of the croplands and meadows. Here, the forest stands guard over the watershed. The protective plant-cover halts the downpour of rain and allows it to soak gradually into the soil.

WHITE-TAILED DEER

Wildlife is abundant. Bears den in caves on the rock-rubble ridges. Turkeys stalk warily beneath arbors of wild grape. Skunks nose alongside the road, ignoring passersby, concerned only with the grub situation. Deer, particularly where the motor road borders Big Levels Game Refuge, miles 13-27, browse within sight of Parkway visitors. Small herds sometimes come for a twilight frolic in the fields around Humpback Rocks. Gray squirrel, chipmunk, and grouse are frequently seen by the forest edge. The great black bird of the wilderness, the raven, dwells on the crags where the wind-twisted oak and pine barely survive.

Rockfish Gap
0.0 mile
elev. 1,909
Access to
Appalachian
Trail (AT)
U.S. 250 and I-64

BUFFALO

Charlottesville 20 miles east, Waynesboro 4 miles west; restaurant; lodging; service station.

Practically every aspect of history or science associated with a mountain pass in the Blue Ridge is revealed in the annals of Rockfish Gap. It has known the cloven hoof of the buffalo and the moccasined tread of the Indian.

The first white hunters came to know Rockfish Gap as one of the better ways through the Blue Ridge. When trade with the Indians developed, trains of packhorses passed through the gap to a chorus of "bells a-janglin' and the long whip a-crackin'."

During the late 1730s settlers from the east began to cross into the Great Valley. They came on foot, in wagons, or in carts with two great wheels that proved equal to the ruts and mud of the early roads.

A French writer, the Marquis de Chastellux, visited the Blue Ridge during the Revolution and noted that, "Rockfish . . . in an extent of more than 50 miles is the only passage to cross the Blue Ridge at least by carriage."

STAGECOACH

Mountain Top Tavern became a thriving stopover for the stagecoach during the early 1800s. A memorable event occurred there in 1818 when Thomas Jefferson, James Madison, James Monroe, John Marshall, and other notables met at the tavern and decided to locate the University of Virginia "in the salubrious climate" of Charlottesville.

Stagecoaches shared the mountain pass with freight wagoners, a colorful, lusty lot given to great pride in the strength and appearance of their teams. The teamsters delighted in bedecking their horses and mules with jingle bells and gay ribbons.

The coming of the railroad "beneath" Rockfish Gap ushered in still another era. It was made possible by a transplanted countryman of Chastellux, Claudius Crozet, a veteran of the Napoleonic campaigns.

Construction of the railroad tunnel commenced from each end. Much wagering ensued as to whether the parts would meet squarely. They did. All this was accomplished in spite of difficult working conditions and no dynamite, mucking machinery, or high speed drills. The tunnel passed 513 feet below the gap, extending approximately 4,250 feet. Completed in eight years, it was used continuously from 1858 until 1942 when the Chesapeake and Ohio Railroad constructed a larger tunnel.

The Crozet tunnel and the railroad were utilized during the Civil War by Stonewall Jackson in his classic Valley Campaign. During the initial stages of the maneuvers in May of 1862, Jackson crossed and recrossed the Blue Ridge to conceal his purpose and confuse the Federals. At one point he moved his army by train through Rockfish Gap to join forces with Confederates in Staunton. From there he commenced his amazing military exploits.

Today, modern highways U.S. 250 and I-64 cross Rockfish Gap and mark the northern terminus of the Blue Ridge Parkway.

Geologically speaking, Rockfish Gap is a "wind" gap, or one that has been formed by a "beheaded" river. Millions of years ago the present Rockfish River began west of the Blue Ridge and flowed through the gap toward the Atlantic. In time it formed a fair-sized gorge through the hard rock.

During the same period, however, the north-flowing Shenandoah river gradually cut upstream through the softer limestone of the Great Valley and ultimately diverted the headwaters of the Rockfish River. To the south the mighty James escaped such a fate, as it was able to cut a sufficiently deep gorge into the Blue Ridge in time to thwart the pirate Shenandoah.

For all its scientific features and history, however, the origin of the name Rockfish seems to be lost with a past perhaps as ancient as the buffalo paths. Old maps refer to it as "Rochefish." There the trail ends.

View of Afton
0.2 mile
elev. 2,054

The scattering of buildings on the front left marks the community of Afton, the last stop on the westbound Chesapeake and Ohio Railway before it tunnels beneath Rockfish Gap. Virginia Rt. 151 heads across the view from Afton and descends into the north fork of the Rockfish Valley. This was the stage route between Charlottesville and Staunton during the early 1800s, and the route followed by Jefferson as he came west in 1818 to confer with his colleagues on plans for the University of Virginia. As Jefferson passed directly below the overlook he rode through the future Lowrey homestead where that toothsome experience in eating, the Albemarle Pippin, was later developed.

View of Rockfish Valley
1.5 miles
elev. 2,148

Through the meandering funnel of the Rockfish Valley flows its namesake river on the way to the James. For a time in the early 1700s the Tuscarora Indians lived by the two rivers after losing a desperate war with the whites of the Carolina coast in 1711-13. After remaining several years the Tuscarora resumed their northward journey and were admitted into the Iroquois Confederation as the Sixth Nation.

Shenandoah Valley

Seen from Rock Point, Ravens Roost, and Greenstone; three overlooks, miles 8.8 to 10.7.

The Shenandoah River forms below and marks the southern end of the Shenandoah Valley. This historic "bread-basket of the Confederacy" extends northward to Harpers Ferry, W. Va., where the Shenandoah River enters the Potomac. By popular usage it extends south to Roanoke, with an assist from the tourist industry. Just as there are many mountain ranges included in the Appalachian System, so the Shenandoah is one of several valleys included in the Great Valley that divides the Appalachians southwestward from New York to Alabama.

INDIAN

The name Shenandoah is derived from the Indian. The Shawnee and others of the Algonquin group referred to it as *shind-han-dowi*, or spruce-lined stream. It is doubtful if the spruce, a native of Canadian climates, ever grew along the warm banks of the Shenandoah, at least within historic times. The hemlock, yes, and perhaps the Algonquin word for spruce and hemlock were the same. Another name source may be the venerable Iroquois chief, Shendoah, who died in 1816 at the reputed age of 110.

Practically all the lowlands within view once comprised a vast 118,000-acre tract known as Beverly's Manor. It was one of the first of several huge grants along the Great Valley assigned to land promoters by the Virginia colonial government to encourage settlement. The authorities were anxious to settle the country beyond the Blue Ridge as a buffer against the Indians and the French. Land agents representing the promoters encouraged people desiring their own land to move into the valley. They found a willing group among the newly arrived Scotch-Irish in Philadelphia. Southwestward they came, on foot or mounted, with few possessions but with great determination.

Within a generation the French and Indian War, 1754-63, ravaged the westernmost settlements. Many perished, many fled, but the resolute held their ground. The victory of British General Forbes in 1763 at the Forks of the Ohio (Pittsburgh, Pa.) reopened the frontier.

Humpback Rocks
Pioneer Exhibit
5.8 miles

Museum; pioneer homestead; information station; programs; self-guiding trail; drinking fountains; rest rooms.

The group of log buildings represents a homestead typical of the mountains from early pioneer days until well into the twentieth century. Held back by the isolation of the rugged highlands, the times changed very slowly. Living in a land of "make it yourself or do without," the mountain man made his living from the materials at hand.

With the ax, broad ax, and adz he squared logs for his cabin walls and chinked them with clay or wooden chips to keep them watertight. The roof was covered with arm-length boards called "shakes," rived from oak or pine.

AX

ADZ

Riving was done with an L-shaped tool called a froe. The mountain man pounded the blunt blade of the froe into a block of wood and expertly pried, or rived, a board of proper length and thickness.

MAUL

On a pioneer cabin the doors rest on wooden hinges, and many of the boards are held together by pegs whittled out of black locust. The floor is covered with thick boards split lengthwise from the center of a log. Skillful builders made these "puncheon" floors snug-tight so that "nary a crack showed through."

Even as it does today, construction of the stone fireplace required practiced skill. Certain craftsmen, known by reputation, were sometimes given the call. Not only did the fireplace have to be solidly built, but the size ratio between the fireplace opening and the chimney flue had to be in correct proportion or the house would fill with smoke.

FROE

The earliest cabins had small "peephole" windows

and two doors opening on the front and back as a protection against Indians. In later years larger, glass windows became common. The cabin in the exhibit represents "that day and time" when Indians were no longer a menace, but a man had to protect his farm animals from the wolf, bear, wildcat, and panther. Accordingly, he had a peephole beside the fireplace, from which he could draw a fast bead on wild beasts pillaging the barnyard.

Behind the cabin is a weasel- and skunk-proof chicken house. It is so securely chinked that nothing but air enters after the roost is closed for the night.

The combined root cellar and "plunder-shed" is a short distance along the path. The lower, stoned section served as a storage place for turnips, potatoes, carrots, and other types of root crops. The ladderlike summer door was used in warm weather to provide ventilation yet keep out the hogs. In the loft above, a man stored his "plunder," or odds and ends.

RAZORBACK HOG

The combination stable, cowshed, and corncrib stands at the edge of the stone-fenced barnyard. Notice the locust pegs used in place of nails, and the wooden hinges. Only the portion of the building below the loft is chinked to keep out the weather. The loft was weatherproofed with hay.

The bearproof pigpen within the yard kept the pigs in protective confinement, particularly when they were being fed corn to fatten them prior to slaughtering. Most of the time pigs roamed the nearby forest and foraged for food like wild animals.

The feed trough is seen extending from one corner of the pen, permitting feeding from the outside. Pigs were removed by lifting the lock rail on top and sliding off the upper course.

The spring house may seem to be a long way from the house. This was often the case. After all, the man of the house didn't have to tote water to the cabin. That was a woman's chore.

The floor of the spring house contains a rock-cased cooling trough of water that helped "refrigerate" such perishables as butter, eggs, and milk.

In general, the family laundry was washed by the spring. Clothes were boiled in large iron kettles, supplied with lye soap from the nearby soap trough. An ash hopper was used for making lye. During the winter the family thoroughly cleaned the fireplace to provide a clean supply of wood ashes. Hickory ashes were preferred. The ashes were dumped into the hopper and soused with several buckets of water. The water absorbed alkali from the ashes and became lye, dripping into a kettle placed below the hopper. The lye was mixed with lard and other animal fat and boiled in a kettle. Salt was added, causing the soap to separate from impurities. After cooling, the soap was cut into bars ready for use. In many homesteads, wash

Stone Fence at Coiner's Dead'nin'

Humpback Rocks Pioneer Exhibit

clothes were beaten or "beetled" with paddles on a wooden "beetlin' block" to sock the dirt loose.

Like the beetling block, most of the adaptations of this "prolonged pioneer" period in the mountains were inherited from European ancestors. The most important, of course, was the log cabin, a sturdy answer to the needs of wilderness living. Apparently the log cabin of the mountains originated with early German settlers coming from similarly rugged country in the Black Forest. Migrants from other lands, particularly the hardy Scotch-Irish, were quick to adopt it for their "hearth and home."

The buildings in the Humpback Pioneer Group are authentic and have seen actual use. Most of them were built about 1880. In 1953 they were removed from their original locations along the northern portion of the Parkway and assembled on their present site.

Humpback Gap
6.0 miles
elev. 2,360

Picnic table; hiking trail; access to Appalachian Trail.

To the left of the parking area, a picnic table stands by the wayside of a bygone road, the Howardsville Pike. From 1851 until the early 1900s it carried wagon freighters hauling cargo between Howardsville on the James River and communities in the Shenandoah Valley.

COVERED WAGON

During the mid-1800s the James River carried commerce between Virginia's ocean ports and the western areas as far as the Great Valley. Roads extended from river ports like Howardsville into areas farther inland. Wagoners from the Shenandoah country brought a cargo of apples, cured meat, chestnuts, butter, and honey, and exchanged them for salt, coffee, needles, soda, gunpowder, lead for melting into bullets, and pretty prints of gingham and calico.

During the hot summer months the wagoners often camped overnight in Humpback Gap, cooking enormous meals in commodious frying pans. Several of the teamsters often joined in an evening of story swapping before rolling up in their blankets.

The large pasture in the gap was known then and now as "Coiner's Dead'nin'." A man named Coiner, like his fellow pioneers, cleared an area for cultivation by girdling the trees, and then planted a corn crop. The term "deadening" aptly described the leafless, skeletal trees. Usually they were cut down and grubbed out as soon as possible. Evidently Mr. Coiner's deadening stood for a long time and became a landmark.

Humpback Rocks
Recreation Area
8.5 miles
795 acres

Picnic grounds; rest rooms; drinking fountains; hiking trails.

The outstanding "curiosity" on Humpback is the rock fence that meanders between the gap and Greenstone Overlook. Reputedly it was built by the slaves of a plantation owner below the mountains to the east. Fence-building made a good winter job when things were kind of slow in the lowlands.

Upon seeing the fence, one wonders how it could contain a hog. Surely the lean razorback variety could scramble over its three-foot height. Yet, hogs in general try to root under obstacles rather than climb over them, so perhaps the fence did keep them in bounds.

The hogs foraged through the forest. In fall they fattened considerably on a diet of chestnuts and acorns. The chestnuts are practically a thing of the past, but acorns are still plentiful.

The forest in each of the Parkway recreation areas contains many of the same species, yet each forest has its special character. The trees on Humpback include the familiar red, white, and chestnut oaks, pignut, sweet birch, serviceberry, and red maple. However, the locally common shagbark hickory and hop hornbean will be seen only occasionally between here and the Smokies.

RUBY-THROATED HUMMINGBIRD

It is interesting to mull over the reasons trees and other plants grow where they do. A large part of the answer is the environment, but not the entire answer. Why, for instance, should the flame azalea be found on Humpback, yet occur nowhere else along the Parkway north of Roanoke?

OVEN BIRD

Still, for everyone but the curious botanist, it "makes no matter mind." Flame azalea is here, so attractively in blossom each May. The more common pink azalea blooms throughout the area a week or so earlier, followed closely by the spicily scented mountain, or roseshell, azalea.

A trail takes off up the mountain from the picnic grounds to a large outcrop of greenstone known simply as the "Rocks." To the more knowing, they are referred to as the "Big Rocks" in contrast to the "Little Rocks" in Humpback Gap just north of the entrance road.

On Big Rocks, 3,210 feet, you are still below the mountain summit, 3,645 feet, but high enough for a closeup of its humpbacked profile and a splendid survey of the distant countryside. The view is predominantly westward across the Great Valley to the Alleghenies.

An odd feature of the plant life sprouting from the Rocks is the abundance of species generally found along streams. Who would expect to find ninebark and alder on a rocky mountain top? Evidently there are water pockets beneath the dry surface.

Humpback Rocks and the open country in the gap were once the scene of an annual Fourth of July celebration. Apparently the holiday spirit became a little too strong, and the patriots curtailed the event.

Now the most frolicsome critters on Humpback are the deer that drift into the clearings "of an evening" to romp and chase each other in graceful glee.

Forest Trees and Shrubs

AZALEA

northern red oak
chestnut oak
white oak
black oak
sassafras
pignut
shagbark hickory
sweet or black birch

red maple
hophornbeam
serviceberry
white pine
staghorn sumac
blackhaw viburnum
chokecherry
dogwood
flame azalea
pink azalea

mountain azalea
huckleberry
lowbush blueberry
deerberry
minniebush
gooseberry ribes
coralberry
ninebark

Ground Flowers

Spring

LADY'S SLIPPER

violets
buttercups
stonecrop
mayapple
lousewort
cutleaf toothwort
jack-in-the-pulpit
bebb's zizia

heart-leaved Alexander
wild geranium
yellow lady's slipper
pink lady slipper
spiderwort
sarsaparilla
bowman's root
early meadow rue

wild comfrey
Solomon's seal
Solomon's plume
four-leaved milkweed
columbine
field hawkweed
strawberry
Small's ragwort
blackberry

Summer

SPOTTED WINTERGREEN

BLACK SNAKEROOT
OR COHOSH BUGBANE

slender-leaved purple bluet
black snakeroot or cohosh bugbane
tall milkweed
spotted wintergreen

beard tongue
threadleaf coreopsis
alumroot
starry campion
gerardia
tall bellflower
daisy

viper's bugloss
yarrow
catnip
horse nettle
Joe-pye weed
ironweed

Fall

bull thistle
dyer's-weed
goldenrod

tall goldenrod
Curtis goldenrod
white woods aster

wave aster
heath aster
catfoot

List continues

Birds and Other Wildlife

CHIPMUNK

turkey vulture
ruffed grouse
raven
crow
bluejay
downy
  woodpecker
flicker
catbird
white-breasted
  nuthatch
bluebird
robin
wood thrush

red-eyed vireo
cowbird
meadowlark
grasshopper
  sparrow
field sparrow
song sparrow
Carolina junco
indigo bunting
goldfinch
wood peewee
crested
  flycatcher
phoebe

black and white
  warbler
chestnut-sided
  warbler
black-throated
  blue warbler
redstart
ovenbird
gray squirrel
chipmunk
cottontail
white-tailed
  deer
box turtle

Greenstone Overlook
8.8 miles
elev. 3,007

Self-guiding nature trail explains Appalachian geology and the greenstone.

The overlook is perched on an outcrop of Catoctin greenstone, a rock formed from a geologically ancient lava flow that inundated vast areas in Maryland and northern Virginia. It forms the predominant rock type over the first nineteen miles of Parkway and is readily recognized by its beautiful deep-sea color.

A large greenstone boulder is balanced atop an outcrop within the overlook. How did it get there? One man's guess is that it broke loose from above on Humpback Mountain and slid down to its present point of rest. The cracking action of seasonal frosts is continuing to break it into still smaller pieces.

On the left of the broad view from the overlook, the handlike mountain mass of Big Levels reaches westward to form the southern end of the Shenandoah Valley. The term "levels" is sometimes applied to a broad, flat-topped mountain area. In this instance the considerable terrain deserves the title of "big." It comprises the major portion of the 30,000-acre Big Levels Game Refuge, George Washington National Forest, and is administered jointly by Virginia and the federal government.

Below to the right at the foot of the Blue Ridge is the village of Stewart's Draft, the home of conservationist Justus Cline. For years prior to the establishment of the game refuge in 1936, mountain wildlife had been greatly depleted. The elk, panther, wolf, beaver, and otter were extinct, and the bear, deer, turkey, and grouse seemed destined for a similar fate.

Justus Cline began beating the drum: "Let's save our wildlife." Largely through his efforts, Big Levels Game Refuge is a reality. Justus persuaded the local farmers and hunters to be partners in the venture. He visited them and

FRINGE TREE

accepted donations, however small, to help stock the refuge with game. The mountain men, who considered hunting as a vested right, now tend to consider themselves "part owner" in the refuge and strive for its success.

A short self-guiding trail loops from the overlook and extends through several moments of delightful forest and plant life. May brings the white tassel blooms to the fringe tree, followed by the purple burst of catawba rhododendron.

Laurel Springs Gap
9.2 miles
elev. 2,878

Laurel Springs flows into Stoney Creek and purls down alongside an old trail to meet the Rockfish River. The thicket understory in the gap is an evergreen luster of catawba rhododendron.

Laurel Springs marks the northern area of abundance in the Blue Ridge for this "red laurel" of the mountaineer. Locally, of course, it is merely referred to as laurel, for there is no rosebay rhododendron or "white laurel" to compare it to.

Each June it blazes forth in a lavish display of blossoms. To some they seem mostly purple. To others they seem more red. But, "them laurels is the purtiest you ever did see, whatever you've a mind to call'm."

MAIDENHAIR FERN

Dripping Rock
9.6 miles
Access to AT

In contrast to the panoramas of the Shenandoah Valley seen from this portion of the Parkway, Dripping Rock stands by a quiet interlude of forest and shade. A short path joins the Appalachian Trail running along the Blue Ridge crest close by. Northward the AT leads to Mt. Katahdin in Maine. Springer Mountain in Georgia is the ultimate goal along the southward way.

Although the forest of the high ridges is far from a desert, much of it is a dry association of oaks with a sparse shrub understory. Spring sites like Dripping Rock are comparative oases of rich, dark earth flourishing with herbs and ferns, wild hydrangea, blue cohosh, black snakeroot, and wild bergamot; goatsbeard throng the moist hollow around the picnic table. At least a dozen ferns are found in the roadside bay to the right of the parking area.

From within this shadowed twilight comes the translucent melody of the veery and the lazy, reedy call of the black-throated blue warbler.

INTERRUPTED FERN

CINAMMON FERN

Rockpoint Overlook
10.4 miles
elev. 3,113

Roadside easel: Catoctin Greenstone.

A "deep" view across Back Creek Valley onto the scabby talus slopes of Torrey Ridge. Rock fragments on the Ridge break away faster than the struggling forest can hold them with its roots. However, the trees are slowly gaining and will eventually hold the rocks in place and permit a topsoil to develop.

Wind-trimmed chestnut oaks surround the overlook.

These durable mountain trees are also known as the rock oak because of their stubborn ability to maintain themselves on rocky, inhospitable terrain.

The local rock type is Catoctin Greenstone, named for its sea-green color and for Catoctin Mountain in Maryland. The greenstone originated as an immense lava flow. As it hardened, cavities, or "vugs," were formed by imprisoned gases. After the gases escaped the vugs filled with various mineral deposits. The greenstone outcrop immediately below the overlook sign contains deposits of white quartz, apple-green epidote, and gray zeolite.

**Ravens Roost
Overlook**
*10.7 miles
elev. 3,200*

RAVEN

TURKEY VULTURE OR
BUZZARD

Picnic table; hang-gliding site.

Here is the land of the raven. To the left a path heads from the overlook to a broad rock ledge, a typical raven's roost. At such places the birds convene in small groups to rest during the day and sleep during the night. The ledge extends over a steep, scraggly slope. Immediately below, weather-carved shapes of rock crowd the stunted forest, desolate and untamed.

Ravens are jet-black birds similar to crows in appearance but one-third larger. The difference in size is seldom sufficient to distinguish the two unless they are seen together. This rarely occurs, as little love exists between them. A raven may be identified in flight by its habit of soaring. A dependable feature, when seen close at hand, is the beak, much larger and heavier than a crow's.

Although they dwell in remote, wild country, ravens do not shun the presence of man. They may be seen occasionally along this portion of the Parkway.

Perhaps the bird most commonly seen from the overlook is the turkey vulture, or buzzard, soaring aloft with seeming effortlessness. Its eyes are telescopically keen for detecting the faltering movement of a dying animal. Buzzards, unlike most other birds of prey, also locate food by detecting odors from the forest cover beneath them. In this endeavor they fly low over the trees in ever decreasing circles until they locate their quarry, usually a dying animal or one not long expired.

The long ridge on the left identified by the bare rock slash is Torrey Ridge. At its base where the Love road and Back Creek run side by side are the ruins of the old Torrey iron furnace. Built about 1800, it led an intermittent existence for over eighty years until succumbing to the goliath competition of the Great Lakes iron industry.

The Torrey was a cold-blast, charcoal furnace with a thirty-five-foot stack. The most exciting incident in its career occurred in June of 1864 when General Duffy's Union raiders descended upon the iron works and destroyed it. During these years the Torrey was owned by the Tredegars, iron masters of the Confederacy. They immediately rebuilt and improved the furnace and installed a hot blast. After the war the furnace declined in importance and ceased to function after the 1880s.

Hickory Springs
11.7 miles
picnic table

Two species of hickory are seen about the spring. The pignut hickory has dark, scaly bark like an old cherry tree. By contrast, the shagbark hickory is identified by curved strips of tough bark shaggily attached to its trunk.

SHAGBARK HICKORY

The shagbark occurs in areas with rich, moist soil. The pignut is the common hickory of the mountain forest, maintaining a roothold in soil fertile or poor, moist or dry. Most of the nearby hickories are pignut. Can you find any shagbark?

The pignut is a botanist's enigma. Throughout the mountains the tree occurs in two distinct forms. One is represented at the spring with scaly bark and football-shaped fruit. Many botanists refer to this tree as a separate species, the red hickory.

PIGNUT HICKORY

The other form, the "typical" pignut, has smooth bark traced with shallow weaving furrows. The hull of its pear-shaped fruit remains on the nut, even after it has turned from green to black and lies upon the ground. The hulls of the "red hickory" fruit split into four quarters and reveal the ripe nuts beneath the tree. The "red hickory" leaf generally contains seven leaflets; the pignut leaf generally contains five.

Why not consider them separate species? Some botanists do. However, all imaginable variations occur between the two extremes.

The U.S. Forest Service (USFS) tree checklist records the two forms as a single species. This checklist is the authority on tree names for the National Park Service.

Other native hickories are the mockernut and the bitternut. The mockernut has large, golf-ball-sized fruit, like the shagbark, but is distinguished by its comparatively smooth bark and its leaves with seven to nine leaflets compared to five for the shagbark. In fall both species are a-rustle with the scurry and scamper of squirrels snipping the fruit from the twigs. After a harvest has accumulated on the ground, the bushy-tails carry them off and bury them for winter.

The well-named bitternut is easily distinguished from other hickories. Its leaf array of seven to eleven narrow leaflets resembles that of the white ash. For a clue, the bitternut leaflets are completely stemless. Other characteristics are the winged hulls of its fruit and the sulfur-yellow buds.

The wood of all native hickories is valuable lumber and adds considerably to the annual yield of the National Forests. It makes excellent tool handles, wagon spokes and rims, and has long been favored for the flavor its smoke imparts to meat.

In fall hickory leaves add sunshine yellow to the autumnal splendor of the mountains.

GRAY SQUIRREL

Three Ridges
13.1 miles
elev. 2,697

Picnic table; access to

Many of the mountains forming the eastern edge of the Blue Ridge were not named from the local point of view. Rather, they were named by people looking westward into the mountains from the Piedmont lowlands. They saw a "three-ridged mountain" and named it accordingly. From our location, Three Ridges forms the right horizon, but does not resemble its name. Perhaps it's just as well. Robust young trees obscure it from view but provide welcome shade for the picnic table.

Reeds Gap
13.7 miles
elev. 2,637

CHESTNUT OAK

During the early 1900s, many wagon loads of "tanbark" were hauled up Reed Creek on the east, to tanneries in the Shenandoah Valley. The bark was stripped from the "tanbark" or chestnut oak in spring when the sap ran high. Black oak and hemlock also provided tanbark of good quality.

Tanning is the process of converting hides into leather after they have been soaked, scraped and stone-polished free of hair, fat, and flesh. The hides are placed in a trough, sandwiched between layers of ground tanbark, and soaked in water for up to several months. During this time a chemical change occurs wherein the hide is "preserved" into leather and becomes highly resistant to bacterial decay. After removal from the vat, the leather is stretch-dried and may then be made soft and pliable by oiling and manipulating.

One-man tanneries existed in the Southern Highlands at least into the 1930s. In company with the versatile blacksmith and miller, the tanner helped make his community self-sufficient.

The tanneries in the Shenandoah Valley were larger, commercial operations. But they have not survived. The last tannery in the area closed in 1979 for environmental reasons.

Stone Fences
13.7 miles

The stone fences bordering the nearby meadows were built during World War II by conscientious objectors. These young men, who were released from military duty because of their religious beliefs, were located in camps vacated by the Civilian Conservation Corps.

Love Gap
15.4 miles
elev. 2,598

One day in 1897, folks of Meadow Mountain gathered to select a name for their new post office. For some time there had been right smart of ill feeling between the numerous Coffeys and Fitzgeralds. The Fitzgeralds were "Tuckahoes" who had come to the mountains from the east. The "Congaree" Coffeys came from the western side. The natural rivalry between the two groups sometimes produced sparks.

Some claim the honor of naming Love for Preacher Elijah Perry, and others say it was Jimmy Sneed who suggested naming the post office for Lovey Coffey, the little daughter of the newly appointed postmaster: "Let's change our name from Meadow Mountain to Love, and forget all our unneighborliness."

It makes a fetching tale, but parts of it are in doubt. Old-timers in these parts recollect nothing about a feud. "I won't say there never was no trouble," says Uncle Jake Hewitt, "but not to my knowin's."

Love, like many an isolated post office, gradually withered on the vine and was closed in 1944. For years it enjoyed a boom on February 14 when young swains came to mail their sweethearts a valentine from Love.

Junction with Va. 814
16.0 miles

North 4.5 miles to Sherando Lake entrance, George Washington National Forest.

View of the Priest
17.6 miles
elev. 2,695

Picnic table; roadside easel: shagbark hickory; trail.

The broad-domed Priest (elev. 4,056) forms the far horizon, straight away, with Three Ridges rising on the left. The Priest is the highest of the "religious mountains," a group including the Little Priest, the Cardinal, the Friar, and the Bald Friar.

Local legend says the Priest was named for an early settler known as de Priest. The names of the other mountains originated in due course from the power of suggestion.

Whatever the source, the Priest and his fellow clerics have been so known for over 200 years.

VIRGINIA PINE

shagbark hickory	yellow poplar	dogwood (early May)
pignut	cucumber magnolia	pitch pine
black walnut	black locust	Table Mountain pine
northern red oak	sassafras	Virginia pine
black oak	staghorn sumac	
	Virginia creeper	

White Rock Gap
18.5 miles
elev. 2,549

U.S. Forest Service (USFS) Trail to Sherando Lake.

The community of White Rock is directly southwest below the gap. It is named for a local abundance of "white rock," or quartz.

Twenty Minute Cliff
19.0 miles
elev. 2,715
picnic table

The rock face below the overlook serves the people of White Rock as a time piece during the months of June and July. The sun drops behind the mountains twenty minutes after the sunlight strikes the rock face. In earlier days, people commonly told time by the sun—and still can. On cloudy days the clock stopped.

Across the valley in the foreground, the steep face of the opposite slope once contained a "hanging field." Mountain farmers sometimes planted a corn crop on land

so steep that the seed had to be "shot-gunned" into the soil.

Hoeing was a precarious chore, its being very difficult to chop the weeds without chopping the corn. Bruised tempers resulted from hoers losing their balance and falling out of the field. A Park Ranger once came upon a man down on the ground, a hoe clenched tightly in both hands. As the ranger walked closer to see if the man was hurt he heard a crackling of cuss words assail the cornfield. "Are you hurt," he asked. The man looked up sharply, then slowly gathered himself into a sitting position. "Ah'm not hurt no way. Ah'm jest plumb put out at this here cornfield. This here's the fifth time Ah've falled outer hit since sunup."

The steep fields have a peculiar effect on cattle. Through the years they have adapted themselves to grazing on the slopes by growing legs longer on one side than the other. Naturally, they can travel in one direction only. A cow foolish enough to turn around loses her balance and tumbles down the mountain. If a cow should miss the cowshed coming in to be milked, she has to walk all the way around the mountain and try again.

There are two breeds of these cattle, this-aways and that-aways. This is important to know during a cattle swap, for it would never do to have the two breeds in the same field.

It's hard to tell them apart when they're calves. A man, "unbeknownst to hisself" came home from a cattle swap with a this-away bull calf. His cows were all that-aways. "The calf were a red'un, but he growed awful blue. All he and the cows could do was walk around the mountain and rub noses passin' by."

You may never see such fields, such cattle, or even a corn-planting shotgun, but "they've been heard tell of."

pitch pine	*chestnut oak*	*pignut*
Table Mountain	*bear oak*	*sassafras*
pine	*black gum*	*witch hazel*
white oak	*red maple*	
scarlet oak	*sweet birch*	

The Slacks Overlook
19.9 miles
elev. 2,800

Picnic table; trail to White Rock Falls.

Forested spurs guide your view into Sherando Lake Valley. The Slacks recall the time when the lumberman harvested the forest, 1916-39. Locally, two long swathes of timber were clear-cut along the ridges. They were referred to as Big Slash and Little Slash. In time they became known jointly as "The Slacks," presumably because it was easier to say it that way.

Like Mr. Coiner's "dead'nin" of girdled trees at Humpback Rocks, the evidence has disappeared.

Bald Mountain
22.1 miles
elev. 3,250

Picnic table

The summit of Bald Mountain (elev. 3,566) humps up on the Blue Ridge crest at the head of Big Levels. The "balds" seen along the Parkway south of the Black Mountains, mile 360, refer to large treeless patches of grass or shrubs covering all or part of a mountaintop. This mountain's baldness has been caused by the restless rock-rubble of its slopes. For centuries loose fragments have dislodged and tumbled down, making it difficult for plants to exist. The mountain was undoubtedly more baldish when it was named over two centuries ago. Gradually the forest has moved in and stabilized the slopes. Even more gradually the rocks are weathering into soil. As yet, many trees stand above a barren understory, but in time the pioneer ground cover of huckleberry, sweetfern, and azalea will assert itself.

The view from the overlook sights the southern side of Big Levels, the long ridge on the right horizon. Several "clinging valleys" crease its broad slope. Many are named for Union sympathizers who hid there during the war: Hite's Cabin Hollow, Taylor's Cabin Hollow, and Zink's Cabin Hollow.

One of their number, Andy Zink, built a cannon and set it up on Big Spy Mountain a few miles southwest. Natives say that he and his compatriots fired a charge of scrap iron at a Confederate patrol "threshing the bresh" for them. Details of the engagement have escaped the history books.

**View of
Fork Mountain**
23.0 miles
elev. 3,294

Fork Mountain, the second elevation directly ahead, is lodged between and almost encircled by the north and south forks of the Tye River. Beyond Fork Mountain, the conjoined Tye weaves through its tortuous valley between Three Ridges on the left and the huge, domed mass of the Priest.

In 1744, an Anglican minister, Robert Rose, established a large plantation in the lowlands seen at the far end of the Tye River Valley. He had previously "chopped out" the boundary with an ax and then returned east to confirm his claim. Here he raised livestock and a profitable tobacco crop.

The parson was a man of many talents. By the expedient of lashing two dugout canoes together he devised a river craft capable of transporting eight or nine heavy hogsheads of "tobo," or tobacco, to eastern warehouses.

Plantations such as Rose's typified the early scene in the eastern foothills. Operated largely by slave labor, each was almost wholly self-sustaining with its grist and sawmills, sorghum and cider presses, tannery, blacksmith and gunsmith shops, and distillery. With few exceptions, plantation folk made their clothes, furnishings, and buildings, and raised their food.

View of Big Spy

View of Big Spy
26.4 miles
elev. 3,185

A "leg-stretcher" trail from the parking area ends in a high pasture known as the War Fields. Across the way, on the front right, is the rocky dome of Big Spy, all but hiding its smaller counterpart, Little Spy.

Big Spy and Groahs Ridge provide a line of sight into the valley of the Upper James with the Alleghenies beyond. The Spys served as lookouts for Union sympathizers.

The War Fields, however, is associated with events predating the first settlers. The high grasslands are so named because of the great number of arrowheads found in the topsoil.

INDIAN ARROWHEAD

This is possibly one of the numerous uplands that the Indians burned off periodically to clear for game. The grasses and sprouts that grew there attracted elk and deer.

HORNED LARK

The War Fields may have known a battle or two but most of the arrowheads probably went zinging after game. It is also probable that the Indians enjoyed the summer breeziness of this highland meadow and frequently camped here, then as now a song-filled homeland of vesper sparrow and horned lark.

Tye River Gap
27.2 miles
elev. 2,969

Va. Rt. 56; west 10 miles to I-81 at Steele's Tavern; east 5 miles to Crabtree Falls; east 19 miles to Va. Rt. 151.

In the long ago, Allen Tye crossed the mountains in this vicinity and settled for a time on the east side of the Blue Ridge by the river now bearing his name. Sometime thereafter he journeyed to the settlements in eastern Virginia and offered to guide settlers into his new found land of opportunity. Tye was of the venturesome few who explored a way through the wilderness for pioneers to follow.

Whetstone Ridge Recreation Area
29.0 miles
elev. 2,990
73 acres

Gift shop; service station; restaurant; drinking fountains; restrooms.

red oak	*yellow pine*	*black cherry*
white oak	*pitch or*	*black or*
black oak	* black pine*	* sour gum*
dogwood	*red maple*	
white pine	*black locust*	

Whetstone Ridge slants southwestward from the Parkway, along the headwaters of Irish Creek.

The wide open horizon view "t'other way" across the motor road looks directly into Maintop Mountain, or Spy Rock. From a prominent rock outcrop near its summit, generations of mountain men have "searched out" the countryside to Lynchburg and beyond.

The prominent high point to the right is Elk Pond Mountain. The native elk that once ranged the eastern forests preferred the higher mountains during the summer. A small pond on a level portion of the mountain-

Whetstone Ridge Restaurant

ELK

top provided them a choice retreat. Neither elk nor pond remains today. The elk fell prey to the hunter and the pond vanished in one of the slow, relentless changes of time.

Hunters undoubtedly named Elk Pond Mountain and it is equally certain that they dubbed Whetstone Ridge. The ridge contains a fine-grained sandstone excellent for the whetstones a mountain man needs to hone a keen edge on his whittlin' knife.

Like all the rock types that form the Southern Highlands, this sandstone is so old that age, "don't make no matter mind." As Uncle Newt remarked, "Hit's plumb out of time, I reckon."

And yet, for all the millions of years passed by since it became compressed into sandstone, it is by no means the youngest or the oldest of the mountain rocks. Just somewhere betwixt and between.

Geologists believe that a long inland sea once covered most of the present-day Appalachians. During the early part of this landlocked sea's existence, sand and other sediments settled to the bottom. These sediments are now represented in Whetstone Ridge.

The rock types between Rockfish Gap and Roanoke compose a geological variety show of slates, quartzites, sandstones, granites, volcanics, and conglomerates infused with minerals and ores.

A local curiosity is the old tin mine a short distance down stream on Irish Creek. The three-storied mine building of corrugated sheet iron stands on the left of Va. Rt. 603, west from the Parkway at mile 29.5.

A series of owners operated the mine from about 1855-1917. The tin-bearing ore, cassiterite, tests about 6 percent, not enough to overcome the expense involved in so remote a location.

But the fabulous-sounding name of cassiterite, and the rarity of a tin mine in the mountains, make the ore a collector's item, particularly for those intellectual hobbyists, the "rock hounds."

Stillhouse Hollow Spring
31.4 miles

Picnic table; drinking fountain.

A small distillery or "stillhouse" formerly stood near the spring. Prior to the Eighteenth Amendment (1919), many legal stills were operated throughout the mountains. The mountaineer brought apples to be distilled into brandy and corn to be similarly fermented and concentrated into "mountain dew." The stiller accepted a pint of each gallon as his due.

basswood or linden	*red maple*
	striped maple
black birch	*pignut*
white ash	*cucumber*
hemlock	*magnolia*

A very unpopular visitor was the "revenooer," who "snooped in" to see that the correct amount of taxes was paid on the liquor. A certain stiller evaded paying a portion of his tax by sinking most of his full brandy barrels in a pond.

Moonshiners were those who didn't bother to acquire a license. To them a revenooer was welcome as a "polecat in a chicken coop." When they met, more than the brew got hot.

Panther Mountain
32.7 miles

Panther Run crosses the Parkway and flows past Panther Mountain just opposite the Parkway on the west. Panthers, or mountain lions, have probably been extinct in the entire Appalachians since the early 1900s, yet recurring reports of the big cats in remote areas of the southern highlands keep alive a belief that the furtive panther still stalks the mountain forest.

The panther is a large animal of exceptional strength and agility. A good-sized male will measure seven feet from nose to tail tip and weigh about 200 pounds. In former days, deer and elk comprised the bulk of their diet. Each cat prowled a well-established route crisscrossing its jealously guarded home territory.

When on the hunt, the panther stalks in a stealthy manner similar to the domestic tabby. But there is a much more awesome strength and finality in the spring, the punishing bite, and the raking grasp of powerful forelegs.

PANTHER

Panthers were never numerous in the mountains, but their secretive habits retarded their "presumed" extinction. Many fearsome tales are retold from over a century ago when mountaineers and panthers met and made unforgettable experiences. Once a man and wife were walking up a steep mountainside, carrying their baby. A certain uneasiness warned them they were being followed. Then, not far behind, they beheld a panther stalking them, pausing occasionally to sniff the trail and glare balefully in their direction. The cat became bolder and drew closer. In desperation the man tore off a piece of his clothing and dropped it on the path. The panther came forward and began to screech wildly and tear and claw the cloth. Soon, however, it resumed the chase. Seeing his ruse work the first time, the man tore another piece of clothing and dropped it on the path. Again the cat repeated its frenzied performance, allowing the fleeing people valuable moments. Several times they caused the panther to pause in the same manner and finally reached their cabin. The man literally lost his shirt, but saved three precious lives.

Other experiences with the panther have shown it to be less than ferocious. One Benny Crouse was feeding his pigs in a section of the Carolina mountains later to be known as Doughton Park. Benny stood atop a ledge and shelled corn, letting it fall to the pigs below. He heard a rustling near his head and looked up to see a large panther on a tree limb a few feet from his eyes, crouched and ready to spring upon him—or his pigs. Benny snatched off his homemade wool hat and smote the panther a hard blow in the face. The surprised cat bounded away in startled haste from Benny and his pigs.

Yankee Fence
33.0 miles

This style is a regionally rare type. Folks say a Yankee settler built the first of this kind seen locally. It is generally referred to as a buck fence because of its resemblance to a series of sawbucks. An exhibit of native fences is at Groundhog Mountain overlook, mile 188.9.

Yankee Horse Ridge Parking Area
34.4 miles
elev. 3,140
Access to AT

Picnic table; logging railroad exhibit.

Yankee Horse Ridge descends from big Elk Pond Mountain and slants across the Parkway to the south. During "the War" the exhausted horse of a hard-riding Yankee dropped on the ridge and had to be shot. The soldier continued on foot, leaving the horse for the buzzards to pick.

Wigwam Creek flows past the parking area, still in haste from its descent over Wigwam Falls. A group of Cherokee from nearby Irish Creek formerly hunted and camped near the stream on Wigwam Mountain, elev. 3,205 feet, poking up to the west. The local whites referred to their camping shelters as wigwams.

CANADIAN OR EASTERN HEMLOCK

The original band of Indians came into the vicinity of Lexington, Va., about the turn of the 1800s. Many of their number were suffering from smallpox. The local militia steered them into the mountains and gave firm orders to stay put. That quite a few survived is apparent from the number of natives with jet black eyes and high cheekbones, tilling their highland farms along Irish Creek Valley.

During fairly recent times, 1916-1939, the mountain forest became the haunt of strong-shouldered men hewing and sawing timber. A logging railway came up the mountains along Irish Creek to the camp at Norvell Flats, directly below the Parkway motor road. One of the spurs from Norvell Flats weaved over Yankee Horse Ridge and crossed Wigwam Creek.

FLOWERING DOGWOOD

A winding, woodland trail leads alongside a reconstruction of the spur, over a trestle to Wigwam Falls. The picture of stream and trestle beneath the sun-laced shadows of hemlock, birch, and maple is a quiet moment of delight and wonder.

Irish Gap
37.4 miles
elev. 2,279

Excellent dogwood in early May.

Irish Gap is the mountain crossing of an old road that follows the slanting valley of Irish Creek along the northwest side of the Blue Ridge and then cuts by way of a small tributary to descend into the Pedlar River Valley on the yonder side.

View from Boston Knob
38.8 miles
elev. 2,508

Trail; roadside easel: birds of the Blue Ridge; picnic table.

The Parkway is wealthy with mile upon mile of deep views, beautiful beyond the telling. Here is a tranquil scene, restful and content to be happy rather than great.

A leg-stretcher trail loops around a knoll that stands over the grassy slopes above Nettle Creek. Log benches by the trail invite you to pause and ruminate.

pitch or black pine	*red maple*	*dogwood*
white pine	*black or sour gum*	*mountain laurel*
yellow poplar or tulip tree	*black locust*	*New Jersey tea*
sweet or black birch	*pignut hickory*	*pink azalea*
	staghorn sumac	*beaked filbert bush honeysuckle*

Clark's Gap
40.0 miles
elev. 2,177

Old Joe Clark had a passel of good lookin' daughters who appealed to the roving eye of a teamster named Sam Downey. Ole Joe took a dim view of his courtin', 'cause he wanted no part of a travelin' man coaxin' favors from his ''Betsy Browns.'' The love-lorn teamster poured his feelings into a song. Far from a woeful lament, the tune is full of sass. Ole Joe Clark go hang!

BANJO

Fare you well, ole Joe Clark
Fare you well, I'm gone,
Fare you well, ole Joe Clark,
Goodby, Betsy Brown.

I use to live in the country,
But now I live in town,
Boarding at the big hotel,
An' courtin' Betsy Brown.

The music made a hit with the hoedowners. Over a hundred years old, it remains a foot-stompin' favorite. The original lyrics have been replaced by countless ''nonsense jingles '' added by countless country minstrels:

Round and round, old Joe Clark,
Round and round I say,
Round and round, ole Joe Clark,
I ain't got long to stay.

Ole Joe Clark he had a dog,
Yaller as he could be,
Chased a redbug in a stump,
And a coon up a holler tree.

The fiddles scrape and shrill, the gittars rhythm and strum-de-dum, the banjoes plink-a-plink. The rollicking music of Ole Joe Clark sets the square dance a-stompin', a-whoopin', and a'carrin' on. The music starts in a fast canter and ends in a runaway.

The young teamster? Sam may have lost his Betsy Brown but the hoedowns got a humdinger.

Like the song, the Clarks of Clark's Gap are very much a part of today. They trace their ancestry to two veterans who acquired grants of land for their service in the War of 1812. Older members of the clan bear the sage features of the Indian, showing their kinship to the Cherokee who settled here over a century and a half ago.

In tune with an old American tradition, the Clarks believe in raising large families. Joe and Charlie, two copper-skinned "sachems," come from a rousing family of twenty-three. When Joe was just a little fellow his mother died. Shortly thereafter, Joe's father married his brother's widow. Each had a fair-sized family to begin with and commenced to raise one of their own. Unto this union Charlie was born. The amalgamated family had a lively time but Pa and Ma Clark managed to hold the line. On those occasions when the older ones took advantage of the littler ones, Ma would yell out to Pa, "Pa come here and put a stop to this here ruckus. Yer kids and my kids is beatin' up on our kids."

White's Gap Parking Overlook
44.4 miles
elev. 3,567
picnic table

White's Gap, crossing point for the old Jordan toll road, lies just north of the Overlook. Formerly the most important way across the Blue Ridge in this vicinity, the local portion of the Jordan road is preserved as part of the George Washington National Forest Road System.

View of Silver Peak
44.9 miles
elev. 2,485

On the left, Silver Peak leads a charging row of tipped-up spurs that leap from the Blue Ridge and dip abruptly into the valley.

Silver has been mined from a few places in the mountains, but Silver Peak probably owes its name to the metallic sheen rain brings to the rocky slopes.

The National Forest road curving in gradual grade up this side of McClure Peak, across the way, is used for fire protection and the removal of timber. It was originally a stagecoach and toll road, surveyed by Samuel Francis Jordan in 1835.

The Jordan family developed a thriving iron industry locally within the Great Valley. One furnace made iron that cannonaded the Mexicans in the Battle of Buena Vista (1847). The furnace became a crumbling relic, gradually disintegrating since the day it fell prey to General Hunter's raiders in 1864.

CATAWBA RHODODENDRON

Just a peep below the overlook is a thicket of catawba rhododendron and a scattering of serviceberry. In April the serviceberry tosses snowflake blossoms as one of spring's first tokens. During May the rhododendron enlivens the slopes with purple.

SERVICEBERRY

Humphries Gap
45.6 miles
elev. 2,312
U.S. 60

22 miles east to Amherst; 5 miles west to Buena Vista; 11 miles west to Lexington.

View of Buena Vista
45.7 miles
elev. 2,325

The "beautiful view" from the overlook, or, as the Spanish say, "Booayenah Weesta," sights a portion of the mountain industrial town, Buena Vista.

It was born in 1890, during a region-wide boom that sought to capitalize on the mineral wealth believed to exist in the mountains.

"Development companies sprang up like mushrooms, each one announcing that it designed to transform some old town or village into a hive of industry, or create a new one. Finely printed prospectuses were scattered broadside, lot sales were held, bonuses were given to industrial 'plants', and speculation ran riot" (Morton, *History of Rockbridge County*).

Originally known as Green Valley, Buena Vista received its present name during the boom in honor of the old blast furnace that produced iron used in the Battle of Buena Vista of the Mexican War.

Indian Gap
46.9 miles
elev. 2,093

We can only guess at the origin of Indian Gap. It may reflect a local presence of arrowheads or it may relate to a few remnant Indians that formerly located in the area. Although no Indian towns existed in this region when the white settlers arrived, small groups subsisted in the remoter areas, at least until after the Civil War. Presumably they were absorbed into the general population.

The Archeological Museum of Virginia Military Institute in Lexington, Va., contains exhibits reaching back in time beyond the Indians of the Colonial scene to a culture of nomadic hunters and plant gatherers. They traveled in bands of twenty-five to thirty individuals and hunted with spears rather than bows and arrows. Some of the spear points found locally and at the Peaks of Otter date from 5,000 B.C.

TOMAHAWK

Licklog Spring Gap
48.9 miles
elev. 2,481

The licklog, old as the pioneer, still maintains a vestige of old-timey ways in the mountains. The "store-bought" yellow salt block is familiar in the pastures, but even now some mountaineer may be chopping out notches from a spring-side "down-tree." In the notches he will place a few handfuls of salt and know that his hill-foraging cattle, sheep, and hogs will be well watered from the spring and can satisfy their "notion fur salt." And when a man wants his critters, he knows where to find them, "up by the licklog."

View of House Mountains
49.3 miles
elev. 2,498

Big House and Little House Mountains hump up "house-like" among the Alleghenies beyond the Great Valley. In the distance their outlines merge into a single profile.

A man of mystery named Shepard lived on Big House Mountain in the unsettled days following the Civil War. On the few occasions when he came to the settlement at Colliers' Creek for supplies, he always paid for them in bright, new coins. Folks "suspicioned" him for a horse thief. However, his bright, new coins were discovered to be Shepard originals rather than those coined by the government. He thereupon discreetly disappeared.

Robinson's Gap
50.1 miles
elev. 2,412

Consider a fine young lad who comes to our shores from Ireland and makes himself useful in the rebellion against George III. He works diligently in the years following and acquires much wealth and a great boundary of land. Then he passes to his reward.

His will, a most worthy document, gives good cause for rejoicing at his wake. "I . . . John Robinson, a native of the County of Armagh in the north of Ireland . . . having migrated to America just in time to participate in its Revolutionary struggle (which I did in various situations), and having since that period by a long, peaceful and prosperous intercourse with my fellow citizens amassed a considerable estate which I am desirous of rendering back to them . . ."

We believe he must have been a bachelor.

The "Spelled"
Hunter
of Enchanted Creek
51.5 miles
AT crossing

The Appalachian Trail passes through the hunting grounds of "Lawless Billy Ramsey." There have been hunters of more renown, but none more true. He hunted with his hounds and rifle, and nothing else mattered. Good livin' was trompin' daylong miles of ridges trailing bear, possum, and coon. And it had to be. Billy's hunting grounds were no part of the everyday world. He lived by a purling spring-fed freshet known as Enchanted Creek.

Lawless Billy had small regard for the "Law." Folks claim he could sleep between two game wardens and still not stay within the law.

Bluff Tunnel
53.1 miles

This tunnel is 630 feet long and is the only Parkway tunnel in Virginia.

View of
Bluff Mountain
52.8 miles
elev. 1,850

As its name indicates, Bluff Mountain (elev. 3,376) rises steep and high, at the head of Otter Creek. A fire tower formerly topped the summit (1933-early '70's), scanning the southern extent of George Washington National Forest and across the James River Valley onto neighboring Jefferson National Forest.

Our National Forests are dedicated to the compatible and enduring use of forests for timber, water, wildlife, and recreation.

White Oak Flats
55.1 miles
elev. 1,460
picnic table

A level stretch of forest coursed by Dancing Creek, predominated by the white oak. This robust, competitive tree can adapt to a variety of habitats; but, as though a tree can show good sense, congregates and thrives in moist, nourishing "flats" where the living is easy. Century-old patriarchs rise grandly above straight and sturdy saplings.

Dancing Creek, ferned and shady, flows like a liquid melody.

Dancing Creek
55.9 miles
elev. 1,300
picnic table

Dancing Creek trips musically with the sunlight over rocks and mossy logs, as do hundreds of sparkling mountain streams. But surely one should be named for a loveliness they all have in common.

The sprite that named Dancing Creek left his (or her) mark in several of these shady glens. Enchanted Creek, Dancing Creek, and the quaint Love Lady that purls blithely between them were all christened with the same magic wand.

They leave the mountains by way of the Pedlar River and are soon lost into the mighty James and the everyday world.

Upper Otter Creek
57.6 miles
elev. 1,085
picnic table

Otter Creek riffles over rocks, smoothing them; pausing at quiet eddies where sculling water striders stroke the water with oarlike legs, sending concentric rings over the water.

Otter Creek Flats
58.2 miles
elev. 1,005
picnic table

Otter Creek, over most of its way, is confined within steep banks. When sudden rain swells the stream it gushes headlong downstream. At the flats Otter Creek rapidly floods over its shallow banks. Clumps of dead leaves show the high water marks of recent overflows.

Why the bare, rocky areas of dry stream bed? Water floods it frequently enough to wash away emerging plant life.

The three-trunked sycamore, to the right of the overlook sign, has an uncertain future. Water erosion undercuts its roots. Winter winds shatter its crown. Rich, moist soil gives it vigor to persevere, but for how long?

Otter Creek
Recreation Area
60.8 miles
elev. 777

Naturalist program: campfire talks, nature hikes, campground, trails; restaurant and gift shop; visitor information; restrooms.

An outdoors interlude of campgrounds and foot trails edges the riffles of Otter Creek, cool with shade beneath a fringe of mountain laurel and a tall arbor of hemlock, oak, and pine.

Otter Creek glides ten miles down the Blue Ridge to the James. The Parkway follows alongside, crossing and recrossing through its crescent-shaped valley. Several overlooks follow the course and mood of the creek as it hurries in its youth and "easies along" in its maturity. Near the James, Otter Creek becomes comparatively lazy and drifts toward the big river. Here the otter once frolicked in the deeper water.

Otter are not now, nor ever have been, abundant in the

OTTER

WHITE OAK

mountains. They prefer large, comparatively deep streams where they cavort and hunt for fish in their seal-like manner.

Forest Trees and Shrubs

PAWPAW

post oak	red maple	black haw viburnum
white oak	yellow poplar	maple-leaved viburnum
chestnut oak	black birch	witch hazel
black oak	black cherry	redbud
scarlet oak	sourgum	pawpaw
red oak	sourwood	mountain laurel
pin oak	dogwood	deerberry
pignut hickory	serviceberry	galax
mockernut	mimosa	
white ash	white pine	
	hemlock	

Terrapin Hill Parking Overlook
61.4 miles

Trails to Otter Lake; picnic and campgrounds.

Virginia Route 130
61.6 miles

Natural Bridge 15 miles west.

Lower Otter Creek
62.5 miles
elev. 685

Picnic table; trail to Otter Lake; picnic and camp-grounds.

A concourse of trees that abide in moist, sheltered terrain flourish by a casual, unhurried Otter Creek.

The sycamore is a tree of the bottomlands. Here, it reaches up and flourishes. At higher elevations it falls victim to snarling winter winds, although a few hang in there with battered crowns and shattered branches. The sycamore is a "moulting tree," continuously shedding its bark. The trunk and lower branches are a smooth olive white, patchily covered with light brown plates of older bark.

SYCAMORE

The black walnut occurs in groves in the moist hollows at the base of mountains, but a scattered few reach elevations over 5,000 feet. Walnut wood is familiar to us as furniture of heirloom quality.

Ironwood is a small tree growing along streams beneath the shade of taller trees. The black trunk has an irregular surface like a pillar of wrought iron. The wood has an iron strength and is used as support for mine shafts and tool handles.

Hercules club is also a small tree with a preference for stream sites, but it seeks its own place in the sun rather than grow beneath taller trees. The upper branches are covered with stout spines, hence the name of Hercules club. In late summer a profusion of white blossoms rise several feet above the leaf tops and readily catch the eye.

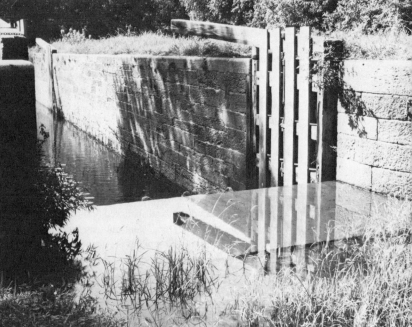

Old Canal Locks

Otter Lake
63.1 miles
elev. 655

Otter Lake is a Parkway token to enhance the natural scenery. During early summer fishermen can cast for trout and bream. The lowest elevation on the Parkway, 646.4 feet, is .1 mile south. This contrasts with the Parkway elevation of 3,950 feet at mile 76.6 on Apple Orchard Mountain.

James River Overlook
63.6 miles
elev. 668

Restrooms; self-guiding trail; restoration of Canal Locks; visitor center; footbridge over the river.

The James River (elev. 610) spans Virginia from the Alleghenies to the sea. Westward the river emerges from its eight-mile gorge through the Blue Ridge. Tenacious forests, underset with evergreen shrubs, cover the gorge's sheer descent to the river. Railroad and highway trim the narrow strip between mountain wall and river. Power dams broaden the James and give it a deep, blue majesty. There is much of the mountain-set beauty of the Rhine. A visitor from Mainz or Bonn would not be surprised to round a bend and see a medieval castle perched on an island.

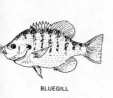

BLUEGILL

Until 1880 and the arrival of the steam locomotive, the James served as a busy commercial artery between the Great Valley and eastern Virginia. The earliest commercial travel was by double dugout canoe, an invention of the versatile Parson Rose (1709-1751). Two Indian canoes were lashed side by side. So joined, they formed a light, stable craft. The dugouts provided a convenient means for Parson Rose and his neighbors to send tobacco hogsheads to Richmond market. Although the dugouts were used for other cargo, their prime service gave them the name of "tobo" canoes.

A generation later, Anthony Rucker invented a flat-bottomed bateau especially designed to navigate the James and carry the bulky hogsheads. Both tobo canoe and bateau were propelled by poling. The latter required a crew of three: one to steer and a pole man for each side.

During the mid-1800s canal builders dredged a waterway alongside the James and ushered in the tow barge. The first stage, from Richmond to Lynchburg, covered 147.5 miles and was completed in 1840. The forty-nine mile second stage brought the canal through the Blue Ridge to Buchanan in 1851. Barges, following the strong pull of deep-chested draft horses, moved upstream with cargoes of fish, dry goods, salt, tar, and plaster. Downstream barges carried flour, wheat, tobacco, whiskey, and pig iron.

Through the mountains the canal fed into the river for stretches of "slack water" navigation. The current was a boon to downstream teams and a bane to the teams moving west. Usually the trips were slow and uneventful. But every now and then the sleepy James swelled into a flood-choked demon and demolished the canals.

The builders of the canal, the James River and Kanawha Company, intended to span the mountains by waterways and reach the Ohio. The flow of commerce between Midwest and East would no longer be thwarted by the Alleghenies. George Washington proposed the plan.

But, unforeseen by the founding fathers, railways proved to be more efficient handlers of freight. Steel rails replaced the tow path. The ballad-singing barge hand gave way to the shrill neighing of the "iron horse" and its teamster, Casey Jones. And then came the bray of the diesel.

Virginia Route 501
63.9 miles

Lynchburg 22 miles east, Natural Bridge 15 miles west. Trail to Marble Spring, 68.7 miles; and Appalachian Trail.

Petite's Gap
71.0 miles
elev. 2,361
Access to AT

Petite's Gap illustrates the changeability of names. About 1740 a man named John Poteet settled at the foot of the Blue Ridge, west of the mountain pass now known as Petite's Gap. His name in early deeds and documents is variously spelled Potteat, Peteet, or Poteat. Early maps refer to the Gap as "Potteets'."

John Poteet was known to his pioneer neighbors as a venturesome fellow, smitten with wanderlust. Two years after his arrival in the Great Valley, he joined four friends in an exploration trip destined for the unknown wilds of the Mississippi region. The adventurers headed directly into the Alleghenies, and after a trudge of some 85 miles came to the westward flowing waters of the New River.

Here, the men decided to travel by boat. Accordingly, they put their long rifles to work and slew five buffalo. With the hides and sinews, and using boughs for framing, they built a river-worthy craft.

At first the stream bore them obediently through the unruly mountain country. But before long it became treacherous with falls and rapids. Even so, the boat of buffalo hide proved its worth, navigating 250 miles before it had to be abandoned. Once the voyagers plunged over a 30-foot falls and their craft remained afloat.

The party continued on foot or boat along the Ohio River. Finally, in June, Poteet and his companions reached the Mississippi, approximately three months after leaving the Blue Ridge.

Life along the Mississippi provided a welcome contrast to the struggles recently endured. Game and fish were plentiful. A measure of civilization existed. The French had established several towns on the river between their big settlements in New Orleans and Canada.

But the comparative tranquility did not last. One July morning the Virginians went ashore for breakfast and were taken prisoner by a mixed force of French, blacks, and Indians. In New Orleans, a hostile court accused each man of spying for the English and sentenced all to three years in prison.

After a miserable two years, Poteet and one of his companions boarded a prison ship for France. On the high seas a British man-of-war intercepted the French vessel and the prisoners gained freedom.

Soon after landing in England, Poteet departed for America. He remained long enough in eastern Virginia to spin a tale or two and then headed for the Blue Ridge and home. The odyssey of John Poteet spanned nearly four years and 10,000 miles.

View of Terrapin Mountain and James River
72.6 miles
elev. 2,884
Roadside easel:
The box turtle

BOX TURTLE

The sleepy-eyed box turtle, or "tarpin," so frequently seen basking in the middle of the road, is suggested in the arched outline of "ole tarpin" mountain (elev. 3,510). The terrapin is an interesting fellow. The honor of having a mountain named for him is well deserved.

He is easily recognized. No other creatures, not even other turtles, bear him much resemblance. His egg-shaped head is set with a pair of birdlike eyes. Most often they blink with the complacency of a lazy hen. The dome-shaped shell is a varied combination of yellow-orange and brown splotches. Each scaly leg has a set of sharp claws well adapted for digging. Box turtles average six to eight inches in length.

The name comes from the reptile's ability to "box" itself within its shell. The undershell, or plastron, is hinged across the middle and the two halves bend upward against the upper shell, or carapace, forming a complete enclosure for head, legs, and tail. The muscles involved are amazingly strong. The shell can scarcely be pried open.

Differences in the sexes are most easily seen by the shape of the rear carapace. The male's is flat; that of the female concave. One who is expert in the ways of box turtles can tell by the color of their eyes. Those of the male are pink or bright red. The eyes of the female may be yellow, dark red, reddish-brown, purple, or gray.

Each spring, with April and serviceberry blossoms, terrapins come out of the ground where they have been dug in for the winter. The first month is spent in finding food—berries, earthworms, slugs, and toadstools—and storing energy for the mating season.

In May and June the males go "a-courtin'." Their manner is decidedly not tender. An amorous male seeks to impress his lady by biting her neck and scratching her face. This attention often occurs on the spur of the moment while both are munching a mushroom or strawberry. Sometimes the female is taken aback and promptly withdraws tightly into her shell. The unrequited male can do nothing but wait and reconsider his brashness. When two males pay court to the same female, a fight usually ensues. The combatants clamber against each other, seeking to bite and scratch. If the struggle lasts too long, the object of their affections wanders away or may go to sleep.

In midsummer the female digs a shallow hole and lays from two to seven leathery-shelled eggs. She covers them with leaves and dirt. Both digging and covering are done with hind legs. The eggs are eagerly devoured by skunks, foxes, opossum, crows, and ants.

The young hatch unattended three months later. They immediately crawl beneath dead leaves and topsoil and remain until the following spring. The leaf camouflage is their only protection from wildlife enemies until their shells become hard.

The terrapin can swim, but prefers water mainly for drinking. When thirsty he often dunks his entire head under water and remains so for several minutes. If necessary, he can live for months without drinking, but always seeks a water hole during droughts.

Terrapins are mostly daytimers. At night they burrow a short distance into the ground and go to sleep. Sleeping is a pastime even during the day; aside from the turbulent mating season, a terrapin has little to keep awake about.

During his wakeful hours he satisfies his modest requirements for food and water and, but for his fondness for basking on the motor road, keeps out of harm's way. Still, this often fatal habit has not decreased the race. They will be thriving when mighty Terrapin Mountain has worn away.

STRIPED SKUNK

View from Thunder Ridge
74.7 miles
elev. 3,845
Access to AT

Picnic table; trail; northern red oak; Carolina hemlock; mountain ash.

Thunder Ridge surveys the wilderness haven of the black bear, or "bar," and of a legendary hunter named "Bar" Tolley.

From the parking area a trail through a woods comes to a mountain-edge platform of rounded boulders. Views from this windy perch deserve the title of spectacular. Twenty-five miles beyond loom the Alleghenies, surging in rumpled row upon row from the Great Valley's western edge. Purgatory Mountain, the home of Bar Tolley in his declining years, stretches out from the Alleghenies on the left. The paired, loaf-like profiles of the House Mountains bump up on the right.

The Devil's Hopper directly below Thunder Ridge is a jumble of rocks so dense with wind-twisted forest that only hunters ever try to live and learn it. On stormy nights, even they are content to leave it to the Devil. Through the centuries it remains a refuge for the black bear. And since hunting bear was life itself to Bar Tolley, he moved in with them.

Even when the sun is noon-bright and penetrates to the

forest floor, a good hunter can get lost in the maze of branches and vines. And during days when fog clutches the mountains in its gray shrouds, eyes become almost useless and ears uncertain.

But Bar Tolley was at home any day or night. He knew the "bar" country more completely than the bears. He knew their tunnel-like trails through the "laurel"—where they led to and how much they were used. He knew every cave they lived in. Tolley possessed a personal knowledge of "nighmost every bar in the mountains."

His home and frequent resting place was a cabin close by on Highcock Knob. Occasionally, he acted the part of the hill farmer tending his corn and "tater" patch. His wife had her garden and children to look after. The chickens and hogs looked after themselves. The family larder, though never sumptuous, was liberally endowed with bear meat. On the few occasions when the supply ran low, Tolley would travel to the valley store and purchase a small piece of meat. Upon returning home he'd give it to his wife and say, "This'll have to last until I get my next bar."

Everything came second to the hunt. What power could keep a man hoeing corn when the excitement of the hounds "baying up a storm" speeds to his ears? "The dawgs has got onto a bar!" Paltry chores are forgotten. Quick, the caplock rifle, the powder bag, and lead balls. His wife hurries him his homemade knife and hatchet.

He is a man of good height, broad-shouldered and lean. Wiry and tough, he will follow his hounds "clean to the Smokies," if need be.

Maybe they'll get the bear up a tree. Draw a bead between the eyes and down he comes. But if "blackie" holes up in a cave, Tolley must go in and scare him out. All he carries is a knife and a pineknot torch. The bear has no stomach for combat and bolts past Tolley into the open. He is met by a semicircle of snarling hounds. They sidestep as the bear rushes them, snapping and worrying him at the sides.

One hound is not nimble enough. The bear swipes it to his chest and crushes the life out. He drops it and crashes away through the thickets. All day and into early evening the bear keeps up his running, fighting retreat. Several times the dogs close in. The bear makes a stand, cuffing and biting them into respectful distance. But before Tolley arrives, he breaks and puts distance between himself and the hunter.

Night brings a pause to the chase. Tolley kindles a fire and he and his dogs "heap together" beside the blaze. No need to fear the bear. His only concern is to get away. Come morning, Tolley resumes the hunt and the bear is brought to bay. His feet, cracked and bruised from yesterday's chase over the rocks are too sore for him to run.

Tolley arrives to find the bear backed against a rock ledge. One clean shot and the bear drops. In jump the dogs to sink their fangs in final triumph.

If his shot merely wounded the bear, he would have met the inevitable charge with his knife. But the bear would only charge to death by steel instead of lead. Tolley did not depend entirely on his single shot caplock. Many times he hunted armed only with his knife. And got his bear.

The excitement of the hunt passes after the black one is killed. Now it is just a heavy load of meat to be toted home. Tolley skins and quarters it, hiding what can't be carried.

Tolley lived a full life, from 1820 to 1902. Today he lives on in old-timer tales. 'Way north to Tye River Gap and south beyond Bear Wallow Gap, they know and tell of his exploits.

One oft-told tale happened near the Peaks of Otter. A local hunter sighted a bear and got close enough for what he hoped was a sure shot. Instead he wounded it and the enraged animal charged. The hunter hurried up a tree, scarcely ahead of those strong claws and teeth. Bar Tolley heard the shot from another ridge. He aimed and fired. The bear slumped at the base of the tree, a bullet in its head.

BLACK BEAR

Another time, Tolley and a neighbor went hunting. They came across bear tracks and trailed them to a cave. Certain that a bear was inside, Tolley told his companion to climb a tree and shoot the bear after he chased it out. Not one, but three bears bolted forth. When Tolley emerged he found one dead bear and no companion. His friend had killed the first bear. But out came numbers two and three—and no telling how many more. The faint-hearted partner fled, and didn't feel safe until he reached home. Tolley didn't mind. He had the bear meat all to himself.

Tolley continually tried different methods of hunting bear. Once he disguised himself in a bear skin to fool a particularly cautious bruin. Another hunter saw him standing by a tree and thought "he had him a bar." As he was about to shoot, the "bar" shouted, "Hey, thar! Don't go a-shootin' me."

But no "bar tale" surpasses Tolley's method of driving the bear home. When he caught up with a bear at bay, he chopped down a small tree and split it at the butt end. By means of a wooden wedge and a length of rope, he then fashioned a hobble which he placed over the bear's legs just above the knees. On hunts where he intended to use this fabulous technique, he took along two small fiesty dogs. They, with great terrier spunk, barked and worried the bear home.

How many bears did Bar Tolley kill? As folks say, "They's no tellin'." Some say he killed one for every day

View from Bluff Mountain Tunnel

in the year. Others claim he set himself a goal of 100 and died with the record at 99. Toward the end, his hunting days over, he "allowed he wouldn't tell a lie fur the last one."

AT crossing
74.9 miles

**View of
Arnold's Valley**
*75.3 miles
elev. 3,700*

Here is a soaring view the buzzard sees. The breeze is cool and brisk. As Uncle Newt says, "Hit makes you feel plumb vig'rus."

striped maple	*black cherry*	*catawba*
mountain maple	*sweet birch*	*rhododendron*
northern	*hemlock*	*gooseberry*
red oak		

STRIPED MAPLE

MOUNTAIN MAPLE

Arnold's Valley lies at the foot of the mountains, far below the desolate dead chestnut trees in the foreground. 'Way beyond are the row upon row of the Alleghenies.

The name Arnold's Valley dates to 1749 when Steve Arnold came and established his homestead. Some years before Steve arrived, a squatter and his wife are said to have set up housekeeping in the Valley.

The squatter was evidently a footloose type who could never be satisfied for long in one place. One day a stranger happened by and stopped for a sociable chat. His possessions included a fine rifle and a gallon of whiskey. The stranger, far from being footloose, was footsore. He noticed that his host had a faraway look in his eye as though he wished he were off tromping endlessly through the woods. He also noticed a greedy eye on the whiskey. And a matter of considerable interest was the attitude of the squatter's wife. She regarded him discreetly but favorably.

So an idea began to form in the stranger's mind. First he offered his host a sample of whiskey, then encouraged him to examine the rifle. The squatter hefted it for the hang and feel of it, sighted along the long barrel, and "studied" the lock. Admiringly he ran his hands over the polished stock of curly maple. The fancy trigger guard and brass mountings made his heart jump with envy.

"Let's have another pull from the jug," said the stranger. The squatter complied wholeheartedly. "Friend," said the stranger, "I'll swap you my rifle and whiskey for your wife and cabin."

In reply the squatter took the stranger's shot pouch and powder horn and hung them from his shoulder. He strapped the whiskey jug carefully to his back. Then rifle in hand, he casually strode away.

(W. Wellington Luck, 1949)

AT crossing
76.3 miles

Apple Orchard Overlook

View from Apple Orchard Mountain
76.5 miles
elev. 3,950

Highest Parkway elevation in Virginia.

The foreground mountain slopes show extensive areas of forest that have been clear cut. Every tree has been removed. According to design, young trees of the same species will ultimately regenerate another forest crop of timber.

The gnarled northern red oaks between this point and Arnold's Valley Overlook have the appearance of an old neglected apple orchard. The fierce winter wind is the architect.

This variety of northern red oak, a native of high rain-drenched mountaintops, is rare in the Virginia section of the Parkway. It is fairly common in North Carolina and forms an entire stand south of Asheville on Frying Pan Mountain, mile 410.

Oaks of Apple Orchard are not as aged as many trees get to be, but some were acorns when George Washington was living.

NORTHERN RED OAK

View from Sunset Field
78.4 miles
elev. 3,474
Access to AT, Apple Orchard Falls Trail.

The gravel road that drops eastward down the Blue Ridge from Sunset Field leads to the former site of Camp Kee-wan-zee, a summer resort for boys. Sunset Field, named by early settlers, was the nearest and best place for the boys to enjoy the evening splendor of the sun.

Gus Welch, a Chippewa Indian and teammate of Jim Thorpe at Carlisle, operated the camp from 1929 to 1951. He named it Kee-wan-zee, meaning "highest," after his grandfather, a chief.

Gus delighted in serving his boys a rugged, outdoor menu featuring rattlesnake meat. His young charges thought it delicious but their visiting parents were sometimes made ill at the thought. Gus jovially encouraged them to try some—with varying results.

Gus kept a pack of four Airedales, each a self-trained rattlesnake killer. They ran the mountains, searching out the snakes. When one found a rattler, he gave a special "yip." Three dogs worried the snake into near exhaustion while the "killer-dog" waited. Then, in a swift, precise movement, the killer dashed in and grabbed the snake behind the head. The others pounced in and mangled it. The killer never relaxed his grip until the rattler hung limply from his jaws. Then he carried it to a place of vantage, tossed it away, and jumped clear. He knew the rattler always had one last lunge.

Close-up View of Onion Mountain
79.7 miles
elev. 3,145
picnic table; trail.

Onion Mountain (elev. 3,811), screened by forest on the left, guides the view into a swoop of lowlands below the Blue Ridge.

Ask one of the folks living nearby where Onion Mountain is and chances are he'll shake his head, "Never heard

RAMP

tell of it." But ask about "Ingin" Mountain and he'll point it out directly. Ingin is the local name for the wild onion, or leek (*Allium tricoccum*).

The plants grow in rich woods soil, often near a stream. Frequently, as on Onion Mountain, they occur in fair-sized beds.

During April a pair of leaves push forth and grow to an average height of one foot. Before the blossom opens in June or July, the leaves wither away. The white flowers bloom in a spiderlike cluster atop the single stem.

This wild onion is found throughout the East from Minnesota and New Brunswick to Tennessee and North Carolina. In certain localities it is gathered in spring and eaten in preference to the garden varieties.

Western North Carolinians know it as the ramp. Around the Great Smokies ramp-eating "conventions" have been held over the years in late spring. Uncle Newt likes to "drap in on the doin's." "A good holpin' of young ramps amongst a mess of eggs, a right smart slice of country cured ham and a slug of corn bread sets a feller up real pert."

The conventioneers make a sociable holiday of ramp eating. A lot of old friends meet, a lot of mountain music is played and sung, and no one pays any attention to the others' rampified breath.

Oddly enough, few of the people near Onion Mountain ever go ingin collecting in the spring. They eat the home-grown kind.

**Close-up of
Black Rock Hill**
80.0 miles

The native rock forming most of the Blue Ridge between the James River and the Peaks of Otter is a black rock known as diorite. It is similar to granite and contains the same minerals, but in different proportions. Diorite is rich in feldspar, poor in quartz, and contains a comparatively high percentage of hornblende, a coal-black mineral.

An outcrop, known as the Black Rock, peers from the mountain edge straight away and to the right. In summer it is hidden from view by the lush forest.

WILD TURKEY

The view here and for a mile south to mile 81 looks into the "Mash," or "Jungle." "Mash" is a local term for a swamplike area. Rich soil and abundant moisture have produced a jungle forest with a dense understory of catawba rhododendron and mountain laurel. Here is one of the infamous "laurel hells" that cover mountainside and hollow in almost impenetrable masses. Hunters and hikers who wander into these depths find wandering out a frustrating chore.

The motor road passes through a portion of the jungle where stately hemlocks rise ramrod straight above the thicket. This is the "Cathedral." When sun shines in slanted shafts through the green gloss of the hemlocks, it bestows a quiet, monastic presence.

RUFFED GROUSE

Wild turkey and grouse are plentiful in the jungle, and

the black bear comes each fall to feed on the acorn crop. The game birds are frequently seen, but the bear has been hunted into wariness.

The present-day black bear is equal in stamina and shrewdness to the "blackie" of Bar Tolley's day. Modern hunters, though armed with repeating rifles, have gained little advantage and consider themselves lucky to make a kill.

A modern hunter is Boyd Lyles of Bedford County, Virginia. "We hunt in the country from Tarpin Mountain south to Headforemost. The best place is below Thunder Hill around Hellgate Creek and Devil's Hopper. That's whar bear run when they get in trouble. There's good hunting around the Black Rocks, too.

"The best hunt I ever had was on Apple Orchard. I shot the bear four times and never did get'm. I first sighted and dropped him at 100 feet. He come charging at me with his mouth open. About 10 feet away I knocked him down again. But he got up and kept coming. I was backed against a rock and couldn't make no run fur it. So I stood waitin' fur him and got in my third shot with my gun barrel pressed against him. That one hurt him bad and he turned and run off. I got him again just as he headed over a cliff. Ain't never seen him since, but a week later our dogs took up his scent whar he holed up. There's a good chance he's living yet. A bar's mighty hard to kill. We killed one down thar one time and thar was a white spot on his liver. I opened up the liver and found a number six shot, wad and all, inside. Been there years and years.

"I usually go hunting with a bunch of other fellows. Between us we take fifteen to thirty dogs. I don't take nothing but my gun and flashlight because I like to keep close to the dogs. Most of the other fellows take up a stand whar they think the bear might come by, and wait thar fur it.

"We raise right smart of dogs because we lose plenty during the season. We was on a hunt on Headforemost Mountain and picked up nine dead dogs. Some were bit almost clean in two.

"Lots of times the dogs cause the bar to hole up in some cave. Someone's got to chase him out. I've gone into many a cave. You ain't going but so fur back in that he ain't coming out. A bear ain't going to hurt you unless you shoot and wound him. But he'll mash you coming out. The best thing to do is when you see a bear is going to mash you is to lay down and he'll walk right over you."

The black bear is not an aggressive animal. Only a wounded one, or a she-bear with cubs will charge a man.

On the average, males weigh up to 400 pounds and the females 300 pounds — all this bulk developing from a set of newborn twin cubs that can nestle in your palm. The birth date is January or early February; the place is a cave or hollow tree. In April, the mother emerges sleepily from her winter home. The first thing she does is quench her thirst — gallons. Surprisingly, she isn't lean, only sleepy. Almost a week will pass before her appetite returns.

The cubs are now five pounds of wide-eyed curiosity and frolic. Sometimes their mother has to bat a bit of caution into them. In search of food they tear old logs apart for grubs and dig for roots. This diet isn't too fattening and by May the mother is lean and hungry. This is the time she might risk going after the farmer's sheep or hogs. With summer and a plentiful supply of berries and other fruits, bears seldom bother livestock.

All bears are fond of honey. Bawling from bee stings and making futile swats at the angry insects, they greedily gobble the entire nest. Fish are another favorite food. One of the first skills the mother teaches her cubs is to swipe tasty trout out of the water. Quick as cats, the cubs seldom miss.

In fall bears concentrate on acorns and become very fat. Their fat layer, just below the skin, may be four inches thick. Before the blight wiped out the chestnut in the late 1920s, black bear feasted royally. Boyd Lyles recalls watching one gathering nuts and eating its belly full. "The bar'd corkscrew up a chestnut and rake down a bunch of burrs, then gather'm up and set beside'm. He takes a rock in each paw and mashes the burrs open and eats the nuts. The burrs was made into a neat, round pile. The first time I seen one of them piles I thought it was some kids up in the mountain.

"Bars have a liking for fat groundhogs, too. I saw where they dug out many a groundhog from the rocks. If a rock weighed a ton, they wouldn't think nothing about moving it. Wrestled it loose just like a man would."

Winter brings hunting season and the gauntlet of hounds and guns. All bears are fair game, from 100-pound yearlings to near toothless oldsters. During severe winters, bears are inactive. Generally, however, all the males of our southern mountains stay out the year around. Females den briefly to have their young. Cubs, as a rule, are born every other winter and stay with the mother for over a year. They do not reach maturity until three and a half years of age.

June is the mating season. The bears gather at some rendezvous along their trails. Here the males bluff and bully each other for their mates. Some rough struggles develop, but mere size and ferocious appearance often settle the issue. Little males shuffle out of harm's way, grumbling, "Wait till next year."

Bears have a curious habit of making claw and tooth marks on certain trees. When one comes to such a tree, he or she snuffles and rumbles regarding the others who have been there before. Then the bear reaches up and adds its own mark before ambling off. These bear trees are proba-

BEAR CLAW MARKS

bly a means by which the animals tell one another of their presence. They also facilitate the "get-togethers" during the mating season.

USFS Road Crossing at Grade
80.5 miles

Access to (AT) shelter on Parkway (right).

View of Headforemost Mountain
81.9 miles
elev. 2,861

Roadside easel: tulip tree (yellow poplar); drinking fountain.

Seen through a frame of chestnut oak, Headforemost (elev. 3,726) eases down to the base of Flat Top, standing aloof and ponderous as a pyramid.

On its yonder side Headforemost breaks abruptly "headforemost" down to the low country seen far beyond.

Flat Top, the taller but less celebrated of the twin Peaks of Otter, was formerly known as Round Top, the reason being readily apparent from this view.

Falling Cascades Parking Area
83.1 miles
.6 mile loop trail to Fallingwater Cascades

The trail descends through a formidable thicket of rhododendron gradually subsiding beneath the shade of a vigorous new forest. Rhododendron, like mountain laurel, re-cover forested areas cleared by fire or timbering where the soil is suitably moist and nourishing. They grow into a maze of leaves and branches flourishing for years until the oaks and other dominant forest trees grow tall and slowly shade them into decline.

The trail becomes steeper and the turns abrupt. Footing is a cautious affair. You hear a windlike murmur and look up. The cascade commences, a sluice of racing white spume plummeting down the wet rocks. And always the welcome of hemlocks, doffing their dark green boughs.

The trail clings downward alongside. A mountain cascade is a moment of wonder. It captivates with its abandon, with splash and swirl, sun-glint and glide. And the sound is a loud, whispering silence where water and wind are the same.

CANADIAN OR EASTERN HEMLOCK

Flat Top Mountain Trail Parking Area
83.5 miles
elev. 2,610

Trail across Flat Top Mountain, elev. 4,001, to Peaks picnic area, 4.4 miles.

Peaks of Otter Lodge
85.6 miles

The Peaks of Otter Lodge is a superlative experience. It has a calling likeness to old-timey days with its weatherboard gray, and the home-folks rocking chairs on the guest porch. The accommodations and menu are a tribute to gracious living. Guests have their own balcony view of the lake and Sharp Top in full profile. High above, turkey vultures soar in effortless arcs. Close by, barn swallows skim and dart over the water.

**Peaks of Otter
Recreation Area**
*86.0 miles
4,000 acres*

Naturalist program; amphitheatre; nature walks; self-guiding trail; living history demonstrations; visitor center and museum; ranger office; service station; hiking; fishing; picnic area; 23-acre lake; souvenir shop; bus trip to Sharp Top.

The twin Peaks of Otter, Sharp Top (elev. 3,875) and Flat Top (elev. 4,001) shoulder boldly above the Mons Valley. The Peaks form the headwaters of the Atlantic-bound Otter River and, presumably, the name "Peaks of Otter" is derived from the stream.

The area is a recreation haven of long standing. The summer climate and abundance of game attracted the Indian. Squaws tended crops of maize, beans, and tobacco. The braves stalked the deer and wild turkey.

White settlers came to this intermountain valley during the mid-1700s. A good road, "for that day and time," passed through the Peaks. It was used during the Revolutionary War to haul lead for Continental muskets and flintlocks. The lead came from mines and furnaces on the New River to the west.

The level valley between the Peaks invited teamsters and other travelers to pause. Big Spring, at the base of Flat Top, gave them their refreshing fill of cold water. A hungry traveler could visit the nearby Woods homestead and get a meal or "bed down for the night." In her widowhood, Mrs. Woods decided to enter the tourist business and became proprietress of the Polly Woods Ordinary. Her establishment provided the "ordinary" needs of the guests. A smacking good menu featured plenty of bear steak, wild turkey, buttermilk, and biscuits.

The ordinary stood a short distance from the present picnic grounds. A dirt road leads to a weather-board cabin shaded by aged hemlocks. Research studies indicate that the cabin may be the actual Polly Woods Ordinary, though bearing the mark of occasional alterations.

Polly and her kinfolk after her operated the ordinary until 1859. Afterwards it appears to have faded into disuse. One reason may have been the more commodious hotel built by Benjamin Wilkes. Mr. Wilkes opened his doors about 1849. He and son Leyburn survived at least one fire and the Civil War. Prior to the war, the stagecoach made a daily stop, July through October. Following the war, Leyburn provided transportation for guests over the bumpy Liberty (Bedford) road in a spanking red spring wagon driven by a black liveryman.

WHITE-TAILED DEER

The Peaks of Otter, Inc., purchased the property during World War I. The corporation subsequently expanded the enterprise and bestowed the classic title of Mons (for Mountain) Hotel. It thrived as a famed resort and honeymoon spa until lack of modern transportation caused it to languish. A fire swept it into nostalgic memory in 1941. The site is marked by a hemlock canopy a short distance north of the visitor center and museum.

An endearing, enduring custom of young lovers is to climb the peak before dawn and await the sunrise. More sedentary souls may prefer to take the bus and go at a later hour.

Hiking trails wind over the Peaks and neighboring Harkening Hill. Parkway naturalists conduct guided hikes through the forest, by the streams, and across the fields. Wild flowers adorn the seasons and songbirds render a melody. A hiker may glimpse a ruffed grouse or catch the disappearing white of fleeing deer.

Johnson Farm

The Johnson Farm, a homestead begun about 1850, has been restored to its appearance of the 1920s and 1930s, a time when the Peaks of Otter knew its most flourishing years. The community had its church, its school, and the Mons Hotel, a genial host for summer guests; some from nearby Bedford and some from as far away as Europe.

Callie Johnson Bryant (1876-1955) and her husband, Jason, farmed the land settled by her grandfather. Jason, an avid gardener, had a clubfoot, but overcame this adversity by planting his garden on his knees and hoeing it from horseback.

Jason worked at a constant pace to improve home and property. He covered the log exterior with clapboards, and surrounded it with a white board fence. He installed a tin roof in place of the colorful but leaky wooden shakes or shingles.

Callie loved to entertain visitors from the Mons Hotel. She sat with them on the ''guest'' porch, shelling peas and snapping beans while they talked. Many of her friends came year after year and reunion time was a happy event. Sometimes they talked until the stars came out but they still kept a-shellin' and a-snappin'.

The Mons Hotel bought meat and vegetables from Callie and also provided work for some of her children. Then the Great Depression snuffed out the hotel and other means of livelihood. Callie had to abandon her home and move to Bedford. One day in 1955, she died in church.

The Bryants and Johnsons still return to the Peaks of Otter for family reunions. They have a special reverence for the home on Harkening Hill with its rain barrel, its kerosene lamps and rope beds, and family portraits on the wall. There's one of Dr. ''Eddy'' Lewis Johnson (1878-1963) who practiced at the Peaks. Folks who knew him can point out the nick in his ear where a horse bit him when he was just a boy. All this makes Jason and Callie proud.

Forest Trees and Shrubs

AZALEA

MOUNTAIN LAUREL

DEERBERRY

red maple
dogwood
northern
    red oak
white oak
chestnut oak
scarlet oak
black oak
pignut
shagbark
    (Harkening
    Hill)
black walnut
    (picnic
    grounds)
catawba
    rhododendron
pink azalea
mountain laurel
deerberry
minniebush
staghorn sumac
yellow poplar or
    tulip tree

sweet or
    black birch
yellow birch
ailanthus
    (Harkening
    Hill)
sassafras
black locust
pitch or
    black pine
Virginia pine
white pine
hemlock
smooth sumac
purple
    flowering
    raspberry
wild hydrangea
American elder
mountain ash
    (Sharp Top)
Carolina
    hemlock
    (Sharp Top)

red cedar
black cherry
white ash
basswood
    or linden
black or
    sour gum
serviceberry
American elm
    (by Big
    Spring)
sourwood
red elder (Sharp
    Top)
winterberry
    (picnic
    grounds)
spice bush
bush
    honeysuckle
    (Sharp Top)

Ground Flowers

Spring

golden ragwort
violet
buttercup
trillium
bellwort

cutleaf
    toothwort
May apple
early saxifrage
great chickweed

columbine
yellow lady
    slipper
wild geranium
spiderwort

Summer
In woods:

black snakeroot
    or cohosh
    bugbane
alumroot

tall bellflower
panicled
    bellflower
gerardia

starry campion
bleeding heart
purple bluet

In fields and borders:

COLUMBINE

sundrop
pokeweed
whorled
    loosestrife
flowering
    spurge

milkweed
swamp
    milkweed
tall meadow rue
wood coreopsis
giant hyssop
day lily

wild carrot
yarrow
daisy fleabane
oxeye daisy
mullein
feverfew

Late summer and fall

Joe-pye weed
clematis
touch-me-not
pale
   touch-me-not
dyer's-weed
   goldenrod

white wood
   aster
wave aster
field goldenrod
rough
   goldenrod

Curtis
   goldenrod
silverrod
white snakeroot
bottle gentian

Birds and Other Wildlife

TUFTED TITMOUSE

CHICK-A-DEE

bluebird
robin
wood thrush
field sparrow
song sparrow
chipping
   sparrow
cardinal
towhee
goldfinch
rosebreasted
   grosbeak
redstart
ovenbird
black-and-white
   warbler

black-throated
   blue warbler
chestnut-sided
   warbler
Canada warbler
chickadee
tufted titmouse
meadowlark
wood peewee
phoebe
crested
   flycatcher
white-breasted
   nuthatch
flicker
pileated
   woodpecker
downy
   woodpecker

catbird
brown thrasher
mourning dove
ruffed grouse
bobwhite
wild turkey
red-tailed hawk
turkey vulture
   or buzzard
black bear
white-tailed
   deer
gray squirrel
flying squirrel
chipmunk
cottontail

Parkway Guide *continues*

Powell's Gap
89.1 miles
elev. 1,916

The Blue Ridge tapers down from the fistlike thrust of the Peaks of Otter and forms a crescent above Goose Creek Valley.

The buffalo came up the headwaters of Goose Creek and crossed the Blue Ridge at this low point. Their road-like trail was used by the Indian and later by the white man as a convenient shortcut between the trading path from the east and the warrior path of the Great Valley.

View of
Goose Creek Valley
89.4 miles
elev. 1,926

The presence of yellow poplar and dogwood about the overlook is an "expression" of fertility. The granite rock contains a large amount of feldspar and weathers into a rich soil.

Northward along the Parkway this soil also supports a thriving association of hardwoods. The ridge southward into the Roanoke Valley is composed largely of quartzite. The forest on its coarse, infertile soil is a struggling company of pitch pine and oak.

TULIP TREE OR YELLOW POPLAR

But the highlands are green and, therefore, beautiful. Below is Goose Creek Valley, bordered by a horseshoe rim of mountains. Forests cover the slopes and extend in floodlike fingers over the valley hills and along the streams among acres of pasture, dotted with haystacks and cattle. The sound of bellowing bull and mooing cow carry up the miles from the Valley to the overlook. Farmer friends are heard hallooing to each other across fields.

Some of the valley homes are white with "store-bought" paint. Others are near century-old cabins, weathered and gray with the blue-white smoke of wood fires curling from their chimneys.

DOGWOOD LEAF

Quakers were early settlers of Goose Creek Valley. The first years of the peace-loving Friends were made hazardous by the tomahawk arguments of marauding Iroquois. The Quakers moved out after a brief stay and then returned two years later in 1758 after the troubles had subsided.

During the time the early Quaker and Indian knew Goose Creek, it formed a marsh over much of the valley. Large numbers of geese and ducks dropped by to feed during their spring and fall migrations.

View of
Porter's Mountain
90.0 miles
elev. 2,102
Roadside easel:
mountain oaks

A long view down Goose Creek Valley onto the out-stretched profile of Porter's Mountain (elev. 2,450), an isolated segment of the Blue Ridge astride the Roanoke Valley.

A fortunate coincidence exists near at hand. A brief survey of the trees about the overlook reveals that all of the common native oaks are represented.

Oaks form the greater part of the mountain forest. Here are six species native to our Southern Highlands: red, scarlet, black, chestnut, white, and bear oaks. The first five oaks are trees of sturdy appearance and regionally

RED OAK

SCARLET OAK

BLACK OAK

CHESTNUT OAK

WHITE OAK

attain heights averaging 69 to 80 feet. The bear oak is hardly more than a shrub.

Oaks are the last trees to come into spring leaf. Those on the higher mountains are not green until mid-June. In fall they are also one of the last to turn color. Some leaves cling to their branches in brown and tattered clumps until spring.

Oaks are divided into two general groups, white oaks and black oaks. The most apparent difference is in their leaves. The white oak leaves have rounded lobes. Those of the black oaks are pointed and bristle-tipped. The acorns of the two types have an interesting difference. The white oaks' require one year to mature, the blacks' require two.

All acorns look like tiny, faceless heads, topped with a cap. The cap of the northern red oak acorn is shallow and resembles a tam, or beret, squarely and snugly fit.

Mountaineers refer to this fine timber tree as water oak, not because of its preference for moist soil, but because of the great amount of water in the freshly cut wood; the green lumber will not float.

Northern red oak is the wood preferred for making the shakes, or roof-boards of the log cabin. The wood splits easily and makes the thinnest shakes. The result is a snug-fitting, longer-lasting roof. A medicine is brewed from the twigs of red and of white oak, for sore mouth. Northern red oak and witch hazel bark, boiled in lard or mutton tallow, makes a salve for burns, sores and eczema. The bark yields a red dye.

The scarlet, pin, or Spanish oak is most common at elevations between two and three thousand feet. From the overlook south to mile 102 it combines with pitch pine, covering the mountainsides. In fall they provide a mid-November show piece. The shiny leaves of the oak turn a rich scarlet and contrast with the deep green of the pine. Scarlet oak also grows in pure stands on the Blue Ridge plateau, occurring abundantly in Virginia and Carolina.

A characteristic of the black oak is its unkempt appearance. Compared to other oaks the black has a snaggle-tooth look. The branching is angular and haphazard. The bark is used to make dyes varying from gold to brown. It is also a valuable source of tannin.

The bark of chestnut oak, a member of the white oak group, has long provided the mountaineer with a money crop. It is peeled from the tree in spring, tied into bundles and hauled as tanbark to a tanning mill. Soaked in water, the bark yields the tannin essential for converting hides into leather. The trees themselves are often sawed into railroad ties.

The white oak owes its name to the light color of its timber. With the exception of the chestnut, no tree was more important to the mountaineer of old-timey days. It served for everything from construction to furniture.

Ed Mabry, the jack-of-all-trades of Mabry Mill, used white oak in his wagon repair work. His mill wheel and mill race, as seen today, are of white oak, it being the best to withstand water wear.

From carefully selected saplings, the basket makers of the mountains peel and smooth their oak splits to weave a variety of baskets and chair seats.

The above five oaks are the most abundant in the highland forest. The dwarf bear oak grows on well-drained slopes and burned-over areas. Along the entire fire-swept (1941) portion of the Parkway, miles 96 to 101, bear oaks form a dense cover with the mountain laurel and catawba rhododendron. Their acorns, like those of the white and chestnut oaks, are a nourishing food for bear, turkey, deer, and squirrel.

Buck Wright and Jesse James
90.7 miles

Buck Wright, man of mystery, came from Tennessee in the 1870s and settled near the present route of the Parkway, just north of Bear Wallow Gap. Seldom seen and moving mostly at night, Buck lived in the Blue Ridge for over forty years. He remained vague about his past but hinted darkly that he was a member of the Jesse James gang and "laying low." He did admit serving with the Confederate Army of Tennessee as a sniper. One of his frequent assignments was to hunt for Federal officers.

Local folks were prone to believe that Buck Wright had some sort of violent past, especially after a doctor examined him for an illness and said that Buck "looked like a battlefield" of knife and bullet scars.

Buck had a penchant for living off his neighbors. By night he visited one farm and borrowed a horse. He then rode to another place far away and "borrowed" a ham, a sack of meal, clothes, or a fat turkey hen. What he didn't need immediately he stored in a cave on Purgatory Mountain, miles from his home. The cave is still known as "Buck Wright's Locker." Once a night's work was done, Buck let the horse loose to wander back to its owner.

Buck spent many hours writing the story of his life in a great ledger book. Some people saw him writing and remarked about his fine penmanship. But no one ever read it. Buck swore no one would until after he died. When that happened, his daughter burned the book, destroying everything but the mystery.

Bear Wallow Gap
90.9 miles
elev. 2,258
AT crossing under bridge

Va. Rt. 43: 5 miles north to Buchanan and I-81, gravel road south to Montvale and U.S. 460.

As with nearby Powell's Gap, Bear Wallow once knew the cloven hoof of the buffalo, making its way from valley to valley.

Another visitor, even to this day, is the black bear. The northwest portion of the gap is a level area about the size of the ole' swimming hole, spring-fed and moist. In summer bears enjoy a cool wallow in the muck.

BEAR OAK

In 1750 the two young men came through the Great Valley on a hunting trip from their home near Winchester, Va. They ranged south to the headwaters of the Yadkin in North Carolina. The hunt was successful and they traveled to Philadelphia to sell their pelts at a handsome profit. Being young and full of exuberance, they went on one glorious toot and spent all their money.

Daniel shrugged it off. There's more where that came from. Let's get ready and go again. But for Henry, once was enough. He meant to stay put and make it in one place. In 1760 he settled below the north end of the Parkway and built a furnace and forge by a stream known as Mossy Creek. Henry Miller, the iron maker, prospered in a busy life providing settlers following in the wake of Daniel Boone an iron edge against the wilderness.

Boblett's Gap
93.1 miles
elev. 2,418
picnic table

Beneath the wind-buffeted branches of a lone black oak lies the family cemetery of Will Boblett. Oak leaves of yesteryear cover graves and rough stone monuments.

When Will lived and farmed the mountains, 'most every family had its own cemetery, a part of self-sufficient pioneer life. First graves were little ones. Burying a child was a grief known to nearly every family. Doctors were wished for but seldom seen. Home remedies and prayers did not always prevail over the many sicknesses of childhood.

If a preacher could not attend the burial, the head of the family read final tribute from appropriate words of scripture. Careful hands placed the coffin in the earth and buried it. A rectangular piece of rock served as a gravestone. A fence, usually of rails, enclosed the graveyard to protect it from wandering livestock.

Each spring the family cleaned away the briars and fallen leaves. Garden flowers or some ''wild pretty'' were placed on the graves. As time passed, the newly added graves of a man's family became less frequent, but longer and deeper. Finally, the parents were laid to rest.

Will Boblett proved an exception to the rule. Will came to this part of the mountains in 1900 and cleared himself a piece of land. He managed fairly well, putting out crops of corn, apples, and tobacco. But the life was hard and the privations many. He lived thirty-five hard-working years and then moved into the greater comfort of Buchanan and the valley. He and his family left seven kindred behind, remembered with monuments of stone.

Among Will Boblett's last words were, ''When I die, don't take me back to the mountains.''

View of
Goose Creek Valley
from
Pine Tree Overlook
95.2 miles
elev. 2,490

Lightning played a prank on the namers of this overlook. At one time a stately assembly of tall pitch pines bordered the site, justifying the name ''Tall Pines Overlook.'' But lightning killed several of the finest and the place is now referred to locally as ''Dead Pine.''

The view is very much alive, however, green with forests and farms of the valley. Visitors from England liken it to their Lake District, scenic inspiration of Coleridge and Wordsworth.

The summit of Harvey's Knob lies on the immediate right and joins you in a broad vista of the Great Valley and the region where Robert Harvey pioneered the local production of iron. The Harvey family operated furnaces and forges at several locations prior to the Revolution and into the early 1800s. One of them, the Harvey Iron Works, was located below on Back Creek, a tributary of the James.

Iron making was a skill adopted from Europe, using the local abundance of charcoal, limestone, and iron ore. Charcoal provided the fuel for heating a furnace and was produced by charring or partially burning wood in an airtight kiln. Limestone served as a flux to remove impurities from the ore.

Blasts of cold air from a bellows powered by a water wheel brought the furnace to the required temperature. Of necessity, furnaces were located by a stream or waterfall. They were known as cold draft furnaces in contrast to the improved hot draft furnaces that replaced them locally after their destruction by Union raiders in the Civil War. According to some known examples, cold blast furnaces were modest structures, consisting of a rock-walled stack usually less than fifty feet high. The hollow cylindrical center was lined with fire brick.

VIRGINIA PINE

Workers dumped loads of charcoal, limestone, and ore into the mouth of the furnace from a platform at the top. Once fired with an initial load of charcoal, a furnace was charged, or loaded, continuously.

The heavy molten iron settled to the bottom of the furnace. The liquid slag formed by the combination of the limestone with impurities extracted from the ore floated on top of the molten ore. Slag and iron were tapped from the furnace at two separate levels.

Tapping a furnace was a main event. The plug was withdrawn by means of a long rod, and the fiery liquid streamed down a sand-lined trough into a series of dead-end subdivisions. Each subdivision bears a fancied resemblance to a sow nursing her piglets, hence the term pig iron.

The Harvey Iron Works included a forge where pig iron was remelted and cast into molds to make pots, kettles, and frying pans; or it was recombined with slag to produce the wrought iron used by blacksmiths. The smithy, with anvil, hammer, and tongs, shaped the heated wrought iron into ever-needed implements, from axes to horseshoes to hinges.

The man who made iron in Harvey's time fulfilled a vital need. For certain he had to stay put and tend his furnace. This brings to mind a certain Henry Miller, a cousin of the restless Daniel Boone.

Hawk Migration

Hawks, eagles, ospreys, and falcons migrate south each fall. Many move southwest parallel to the Blue Ridge, taking advantage of the lift provided by warm air currents, or thermals, rising up the mountainsides.

Most numerous and readily seen are the broad-winged hawks and the red-tailed hawks, traveling singly or in small groups. Broad-wings pass through from mid-September to mid-October, red-tails from mid-October to mid-November.

A good time for hawk watching is the forenoon of days with sunshine and scattered cumulous clouds. Hawks leave their overnight perches as they feel the newly warmed air reaching up the mountain slopes. The hawks spiral upward on the flow of warm air expanding from the valleys, as high as the air's buoyancy will carry them. Then they peel off and glide swiftly out of sight. Eventually they lose elevation and make another vertical ascent up a thermal.

Where are they going? The broad-wing goes south, from Central America to Chile. The red-tail winters from the southern United States to central Mexico.

View of Purgatory Mountain
92.2 miles
elev. 2,415
Roadside easel: hawk migration

The huge prominence rising above the Great Valley is Purgatory Mountain (elev. 3,031). Buchanan town clusters at its base with the James River meandering by like a sky-blue ribbon. Buchanan dates to the early 1740s when an adventurous sea captain named Patton forsook the salt spray and became a land promoter, inducing groups of Ulster Scots to settle along the upper James.

John Buchanan was his partner and son-in-law. Twin settlements were named for these men, Pattonsburg on the north bank, Buchanan on the south. The son-in-law's namesake outgrew the father-in-law's. Now both are one and the same—Buchanan.

The "Carolina" road, extending southwest along the Great Valley from Philadelphia, passed through the town. Patton received a commission from the colonial government to lay planks on the local road as part of an early improvement program.

COVERED WAGON

Over its rough path came lurching stagecoaches and wagons. Just north of town the road forded a horseshoe bend of a tributary near its entry into the James. This fording was a wallowing, strenuous undertaking and often required the strength of additional teams. Drivers referred to the ordeal as "going through Purgatory."

The tributary became known as Purgatory Creek and gave its name to the mountain from which it flows.

View of Sharp Top
92.6 miles
elev. 2,415

Framed by a stand of oak, hickory, and dogwood, Sharp Top (elev. 3,870) is the dominant elevation seen on the far side of Goose Creek Valley and offers a fine view for photographers.

**View of
Montvale Town
in
Goose Creek Valley**
95.9 miles
elev. 2,441
U.S. 460

Montvale formerly bore the name of Bufordsville in honor of a capricious gentleman who gave land to the Norfolk & Western Railway on condition that passenger trains always stop at the station. This was very gallant but rather impractical when there were no passengers. The Norfolk & Western Railway lived up to the agreement for a long time but now just toots a whistle—maybe.

**Two Views of
Iron Mountain
Hollow**
96.4 miles
elev. 2,375

Shortly after the Civil War the Southern Highlands were extensively prospected and mined for iron ore. Northern and European capitalists invested large sums of money. Many ore samples showed an iron content considered high at the time.

Iron had been produced within and near the mountains since the last half of the eighteenth century, but lack of transportation and other factors limited development. However, the postwar industrial boom created a huge demand. Railways and canal barges were now available to move the ore and iron.

Locally, mines operated on both sides of the Blue Ridge. Ore was withdrawn from drift mines, dug at a slight upward tilt into the mountain. Miners worked the ore loose with air drills, picks, and shovels. Mules hauled empty ore cars into the mines, then retraced their steps for more empties. The loaded cars rolled unaided down tracks to an unloading zone where workmen tipped the contents into gondolas. In these cars the ore was hauled by dinkey engine to a pit and dumped in. A stream of water, released from a dam, washed away the loose dirt.

Workmen reloaded the ore into gondolas located on railroad spurs which led into the main line. Ore went to two blast furnaces in Roanoke, or sometimes further southwest to Radford and Pulaski. The pig iron from these plants was then shipped to northern steel mills.

The anticipated future for the Blue Ridge industry never materialized. The greatest reason for its failure occurred in 1892 with the discovery of the fantastically rich and easily worked Mesabi mines of Minnesota.

The local mines closed down one by one. Five miles south and on the opposite slope of the Blue Ridge is the abandoned site of the Edith mine. It produced from 1880 to 1920 and was one of the last in operation. The mine still has plenty of black "speckled" ore, but of low (35 percent) grade. At its peak it had an output of 300 tons a day and employed 150 men.

**View of
Taylor's Mountain**
97.0 miles
elev. 2,365
AT Crossing

Beyond the garland of chestnut oak edging the overlook, Taylor's Mountain stands at the end of the long mountain wall forming the yonder side of Goose Creek Valley.

The overall wealth of greenness obscures the final decay of charred tree trunks, now fallen and moldering into soil. But for decades the relics of burned trees marked the grave of a forest.

On April 6, 1942, a farmer in Goose Creek Valley set one of his fields afire to "burn off the bresh." April in the mountains is tinder-dry, without the fireproofing of new green that May coaxes forth.

This particular April, wind carried the flames beyond the farmer's control.

High on Sharp Top, in the old fire tower, a guard saw smoke and notified the Parkway's rangers and the foresters of Jefferson National Forest. The fire was still small, not more than two acres.

Rough terrain and roundabout roads delayed the attack for an hour. Now the fire covered a hundred acres, growing from a creeping brush fire to a crown fire, leaping from tree to tree.

More help arrived from organized crews and volunteers. Men sweated with axes, bush hooks, and fire rakes, clearing a line ahead of the blaze. Others manned pumps and shot water into the flames. The efforts of six hundred men finally brought the fire under control after it had ravaged the forest for two days and nights.

Then followed the arduous mopping up. Ax men cut open smoldering logs and stumps. Fire fighters with backpack pumps sprayed the glowing embers. When it was all over, 10,300 acres of land lay desolate.

There is no way accurately to assess the damage. The mountains are green again and only a few charred snags recall the tragedy. Fire burns more than trees. Topsoil, with its millions of organisms vital to plant and animal life, is destroyed.

On these rocky slopes, the soil is poor and the essential humus develops slowly. Fires condemn the scenery to scrawny forests studded with the funereal relics of trees that used to be.

PAULOWNIA TREE

Paulownia Tree

The Paulownia is seen at points along the motor road over the Roanoke Valley. It is conspicuous for its large heartshaped leaves. The flowers form in autumn without a bud cover. In spring they expand into large lavender blossoms resembling the related snapdragon.

The tree is native of China, introduced to America as an ornamental by way of Europe.

Black Horse Gap
97.7 miles
elev. 2,402

Jefferson National Forest Service Road access to (AT) and shelter

The stillness is broken by the dry, crackling sound of steel rims grating into the rocky road. The harsh cry of the stage driver urging the horses carries to the lonely mountain crest at Black Horse Gap.

The last mile is slowly gained and a coal-black foursome of sweat-slick horses rounds the final bend. The stage run from West Virginia is a wearisome venture.

The driver reins up for a breather in the Gap and leans down to the passengers. "We made'er, Guvner. The rest is all down hill." They nod back with limp enthusiasm. A crack of the whip and the stage moves on. "We'll all get to stretch our legs directly," yells the driver. "The tavern's just ahead."

A quarter mile down the east side of the Blue Ridge the stage comes to a welcome halt at the Mountain Gate Toll House. Stiffness makes its painful, unlamented exit. Then comes the pleasure to stretch, breathe in the breeze, and drink deeply from the spring. A chunky traveler sighs as he wipes a sleeve across his chin, "Best water a man ever drunk."

STAGECOACH

The driver, busy unhitching the horses, pauses as the tavern keeper walks up. "Got a heavy load of mail this trip. I didn't know they was that many folks could read, much less write." "That so?" comes the noncommittal reply. "How'd Star make out this trip?" "He done tolerable. Pulled his share far as I could tell. Reckon he'll get swapped off, though. Once a horse comes down with the colic, this life gets too rough fur'em."

The men lead the horses to a shelter for rest and feed. "A good-natured horse," says the tavern keeper, patting Star on the neck. "Wouldn't mind havin' him myself."

A fresh team is hitched up, the passengers reload, and the stage sallies off, crunching and hunching down the mountain.

The tavern keeper walks to a tilted rock shelf. From this picturesque lookout he places a horn to his lips and sounds six strident blasts. Several miles below, Paschal Buford gets the message and prepares a supper of fried chicken and biscuits for six incoming guests. They'll be right on time unless a wheel breaks or a horse goes lame.

View of the Great Valley
99.6 miles
elev. 2,493
picnic table

For a hundred miles south from Rockfish Gap the Parkway skims above the Great Valley, the great swath that bisects the entire Appalachian system. Once the byway of the Indian warrior and the pioneer, it now carries a pulsing mainline of commerce and travel.

The roads over the valley are constantly maintained and improved. But during Robert Looney's day, 200 and more years ago, roads were rough and uncertain for anything on wheels. Looney ran a gristmill at a ford where the stream bearing his name flows into the James. As Mr. Kegley, the assiduous historian of this region remarks, "A good part of the time, the river was past fording." Times have changed.

Take a good look at this view and drink it in. Say farewell (or hello) to the Great Valley and Alleghenies.

View of the Quarry
100.9 miles
elev. 2,170

Over most of its Blue Ridge cruise, the Parkway rides atop the crestline, the high backbone of the range. For its entry into the Roanoke Valley the Parkway chooses a more gradual descent. The Blue Ridge crestline is seen on the left, breaking abruptly down to Buford's Gap.

On the right a seven-mile "island" of the Blue Ridge extends toward the Roanoke River.

Buford's Gap is not really a low pass over the mountains, but an actual break-through. From the east the Indian Trading Path came by way of the gap and joined the Warrior Path at the present site of Roanoke. Both paths became the routes of pioneers and now carry major railroads and highways.

The excavation pit seen below is a dolomite quarry. Dolomite is a rock similar to limestone, but with a heavy percentage of magnesium. This dolomite contains approximately 20 percent magnesium.

The quarry began operations in 1916 and since that date has maintained an annual output of 6 to 7 million tons. The stone is removed on an endless three-quarter-mile-long belt to the fine crushers at the company plant. The product is used in making concrete and building blocks, and as gravel for railroad ballast and highways.

In character with most limestone and dolomite deposits, this one is hollowed by several caves, containing the cone-shaped stalactites and stalagmites, and a few sleepy bats.

Geologically, the stone is known as shady dolomite, formed during the early Cambrian period, some half-billion years ago. During this time the Blue Ridge region lay beneath a narrow sea extending from Nova Scotia to the Gulf of Mexico. The dolomite was deposited as a sediment on the bottom of the sea.

U.S. Highway 460
105.8 miles

Bedford 21 miles east, Lynchburg 46 miles east, Roanoke 9 miles west.

Norfolk & Western Railway (N & W)
106.9 miles
elev. 1,161

Not long ago the magnificent charge of the steam engine thundered through from Buford's Gap. No sight or sound breathed more excitement than the rhythmic power of the drive wheels and the shrill whistle with its plume of steam.

Now the diesel has replaced the coal burner. But the farewell was a proud one. During the final runs, railroad buffs lined the rails at every stop to wave, to cheer, and gather snapshot memories.

Work crews laid the first rails through this region of the Blue Ridge in 1852 and completed the line from Lynchburg, Va., to Bristol, Tenn., in 1856. Known as the Virginia and Tennessee, it was the quickest route to New Orleans and on to the California gold fields by way of the Panama Canal.

The present N. & W. is the result of two receiverships in the late 1880s. In 1883 the N. & W. shipped the first carload of high-quality coal from West Virginia to Norfolk. The chief traffic category of the road remains coal. More than 70 million tons are shipped annually and the future promises more. The rails are busy. They glisten in the sun.

Bluebirds and Apples

APPLE BLOSSOM

Some things pass without regret, but not the bluebird. Year after year its numbers diminish and in some places where it was once common it is seen no more. The bluebird was once as familiar as apple blossoms, and each a compliment to the other. The bluebird adapted well to the family farm and the apple orchard where the trees were tended casually and the apples sometimes wormy. They nested in holes in old apple trees where a branch had rotted out, or a woodpecker had drilled a hole.

BLUEBIRD

Orchards are forest-size now, maintained in orderly rows, pruned, fertilized, and sprayed to kill insect pests that once fed bluebirds. The apples are beautiful, bountiful, toothsome, and aseptically edible.

Have insecticides done in the bluebird? Perhaps. But we are seeing a more knowledgeable and restrained use of insecticides, and surely the bluebird is coming back. The Parkway is helping out. Nesting boxes are located on roadside fenceposts for several miles north and south. Some are occupied by bluebirds. We can have apples and bluebirds too.

Read Mountain
109.5 miles

David Read came from east in Henrico County about 1840. The mountain named for him forms the long profile on the straightaway horizon. Seen from your vantage with a foreground of rolling pasture and rail fence, time has not changed much since farmer David's day. Mourning doves, singly or in twos, fly back and forth over the clearings. A bluebird carols soft notes from a nearby post.

But sometimes today's sounds reach from U.S. 460, busy but unseen, with the high-pitched hum of speeding tires and the hoarse, straining gutturals of engines and gears.

It's a relaxation to have a parkway to lazy along and not be in a hurry.

Stewarts Knob
Parking Overlook
110.6 miles
elev. 1,275
trail

At Stewarts Knob the Blue Ridge builds into a final surge of 2,470 feet and then subsides into the Roanoke Valley. For five miles south the crestline is carried by a series of middlin' hills to the river's edge.

Further southward the Blue Ridge again rises into mountains that form the high eastern rim of the rolling upland known as the Blue Ridge plateau.

Progressing southward the Blue Ridge gradually

increases in stature and the plateau becomes more mountainous until—from Grandfather Mountain and beyond—it resolves into a green sequence of high ranges and deep valleys.

irginia Highway 24
112.2 miles

Roanoke 4 mile west (nearest exit)

Roanoke River Bridge
114.8 miles
river elev. 824

Roanoke River Parking Overlook
114.9 miles
elev. 985
trail

A path travels from the overlook beneath the 1000 foot bridge to a balcony view of the Roanoke River.

Originally the river had three names. The upper region you witness here was known as Goose Creek. The middle portion through the piedmont was once known as the Staunton. The name Roanoke formerly applied only to the section through North Carolina leading to the Atlantic at Albemarle Sound. This invites the thought that people first settling along the upper portions of the river didn't know its ultimate destination.

Roanoke, like the well-known wampum, is an Indian word for money. The currency occurred naturally in the form of flat shells found in the tidewater region.

From the balcony view, the Roanoke glides meekly beneath its forest cover. The modest size is often swelled by spring rains and summer flash storms.

A red brick water-gauging station a short distance upstream keeps check on the flow rate for the Appalachian Power Company. A dependable water supply is required to produce the steam essential in generating electricity.

The single rail track following alongside the Roanoke illustrates the romance of rivers and railroads. The smooth grade of the stream provides the least strenuous path through the mountains. This is the path followed by the coal-hauling Norfolk & Western gondolas.

MOURNING DOVE

Scenic Four-Mile Loop Over Roanoke Mountain
120.3 miles

No recreation vehicles over 20 feet long; 7 overlooks; 10-minute trail; exhibit identifying local mountains.

A balcony view reveals greater Roanoke as though it were in the palm of your hand. You see it now, spreading over a gentle valley, encircled by mountain greenery. The residences are well tended and neatly arrayed. The city center has clean buildings that form a skyline of modest height. New construction and a steady flow of traffic indicate a thriving present. Turn back in time and see the making of a city.

Two great natural pathways, known to buffalo herds and to Indians, converged in the Roanoke Valley. One trail came from the east through an easy passage in the Blue Ridge and joined a trail traversing southwest along the Great Valley from New York to Tennessee.

In the 1740s settlers established homesteads in the Roanoke Valley and gradually commenced a trade with the flow of travelers along the pathways. They produced a surplus of corn; they made salt; they made iron.

CHINQUIPIN

The trails became major routes for freight wagon and stage coach. The Roanoke Valley became a hub of commerce.

But until the 1880s, the name of Roanoke referred to the river. Local maps did show a little-known site called Big Lick, but urban development centered in the nearby municipality of Salem.

The 1880s were a time of ferment. A revitalized iron industry was commencing in the valley, using native ore and limestone. The new furnaces needed coke to fuel the hot air blast. Coke came from coal and coal came on the railroads.

CHESTNUT

The railroads were expanding. A line was under construction coming southwest along the Great Valley from Maryland. Where would it join the established east-west line? Big Lick, at the junction of the old Indian trails, was the logical choice.

In 1882 Big Lick became Roanoke, named for the river, which in turn derived from an Indian word for seashells used as trading tokens.

The railroads attracted other industries and growth so rapid that the citizens pridefully referred to their Roanoke as the Magic City. Through the years, Roanoke has remained a "railroad town," the corporate center of the Norfolk & Western Railway.

Mindful of this heritage, the Roanoke Transportation Museum displays "the South's largest collection of fabled 'Iron Horses' of steam railroading days."

The future of Roanoke is secure, riding the great trails of the past.

**Mill Mountain
Spur Road**
120.5 miles

1 mile to Roanoke Mountain campground. Road continues to Mill Mountain Park, Children's Zoo, and City of Roanoke.

Campers or picnickers with some time to enjoy can travel to nearby Mill Mountain for a daytime visit to the Children's Zoo. The zoo is a stroll through Mother Goose Land with The Cow That Jumped over the Moon, Mary's Little Lamb, and The Little Piggie That Went to Market.

But first let's take a look around, and later in the evening join the big campfire circle to hear tales both tall and true.

The spur road runs the crest of Chestnut Ridge. A map at Chestnut Ridge overlook shows the 5.4 miles of foot trails voyaging the area.

POISON IVY

Forest Trees

Mixed hardwoods and pine with sourwood and oaks predominating:

sourwood	pignut	paulownia or
white oak	yellow poplar or	princess tree
chestnut oak	tulip tree	mimosa
scarlet oak	butternut	black or
black oak	black cherry	pitch pine
red oak	black locust	Table Mountain
blackjack oak	sassafras	pine
sour or	red maple	Virginia pine
black gum	dogwood	chestnut sprouts
mockernut	ailanthus	chinquapin

Did you ever see so many vines? All kinds of vines, wild grape, Virginia creeper, honeysuckle, and watch out for poison ivy. The vines cover the ground six feet deep. They climb up and over the trees, dripping from the branches, weaving a green roof among the treetops. But the vines never encumber the trails or the campgrounds.

SOURWOOD

Chestnut trees once grew abundantly on the ridge until the big trees were killed by fungus blight in the late 1920s. Schoolboys came to the ridge each fall to gather the sweet-tasting nuts. Chestnut sprouts, rising from the roots of old trees, still persist. Some reach a height of twenty feet and may even flower and produce nuts, but always they succumb to the still virulent blight.

The schoolboys are now granddaddies. They have another fine memory of Chestnut Ridge. They came and played at the abandoned site of an iron ore mine. The excavations are still evident along the trails. No other identifying vestige remains. The dinkey engine made a last trip and the workers packed their picks and shovels and led the mules away. The mine shafts caved in and filled with dirt, and the forest took over.

VIRGINIA PINE

There are great stories to relive at the campfire circle. Ore from Chestnut Ridge fed the cold blast furnace of Robert Harvey, operating in the Roanoke Valley before 1800. His was a small beginning compared to the larger, more efficient hot blast furnaces in the Roanoke Valley of 1880 to 1920. This was the time of the dinkey engine and its haul of ore-filled gondolas rolling through the city of Roanoke. Iron making became a major industry in west-

Roanoke River

ern Virginia and thrived until improved technology and accessibility to high-grade ores concentrated the industry in the Great Lakes region. The winds of change. Whither will they blow?

U.S. 220
121.4 miles

Roanoke 4 miles north; Rocky Mount, Va., 19 miles south.

Ode to an Agronomist

Morning rubbed its eyes and stretched over the Blue Ridge community of Sparta, North Carolina. Roosters crowed their prideful dawn salute. Dairy cattle bawled hungry eagerness as they headed for pasture. Farmers hefted ten-gallon milk cans into cooling water, then trudged to house and breakfast. Back in 1950 it was the start of another midsummer day.

Bill Hooper, the Blue Ridge Parkway Agronomist, bade farewell to his host at Kelly's Motel and motored to a section of farmland within the Parkway right-of-way. This morning he was checking on land leased to local farmers between his entry on the Parkway at Roaring Gap, and then southward into dusk and the call of the whip-poor-will.

He parked his government car and strode to a bordering snake-rail fence. Per usual he paused to pull some tall grass; then slowly munching a stem, he leaned on the fence to ponder the land's progress or lack of it.

His blue eyes brightened. Chalky streaks banded a somewhat jaundiced pasture, indicating a recent and needed application of lime. A wide, white smile gleamed on his sunburned face. Good. Harvey Wilson had kept his word.

Harvey had asked for another chance to retain his lease with the Parkway. He'd slipped a bit once he had use of the land. He took off the hay, but he didn't lime or fertilize. "My daddy didn't do none of that, and I learned my farming from my daddy." Bill, with polite firmness, said he might have to cancel the lease. "Mr. Cooper," said a mite anxious Harvey, "You just give me another chance. I give you my word."

Mr. Cooper? Bill never could tell why, but the mountain farmers often called him Cooper instead of Hooper. Bill didn't mind. Call me Cooper and let's come to an agreement.

Bill stretched a happy stretch. There, profiled on the hillside, he was the prototype mountaineer, square-shouldered, lean, and sinewy.

In anticipation of further good findings, he vaulted the fence and crossed to a steep crease in the land. A recent red scar of bare erosion was now tended by a packing of stones and brush. Rain torrents could no longer gouge away the soil. Green sod was closing and healing the wound.

And now for that broken down section of fence. Bill had supplied Harvey with some of his "scrounged-from-high-and-low" stock of chestnut rails. Yes, Harvey had removed and replaced the broken sections.

A year ago, Harvey signed a five-year lease. For the modest sum of $1.00 per acre per year he agreed to specified land use practices. He gradually backslid some, but now with his word and a handshake, the agreement was secure.

This was true of Harvey and the mountain people in general. Giving one's word was more binding than a signature. Of course most farmers fulfilled their agreement without any prodding, but then, there's some Harvey in the best of us. Most importantly, the lease was in good hands and so was the farmland scenery.

Bill returned to his car and headed south. Foster Caudill at Laurel Gap wanted to put more sheep in his leased pasture. Bill felt sure he could work something out. Foster was a good farmer and his tending produced a lush growth that the sheep never overgrazed.

Things were in pretty good shape. Parkway neighbors were, by and large, cooperative and recognized that they had a good deal. "Yes," mused Bill, "things have shaped up very well. But it wasn't always that way. No sir. What a time I had when I first started. . . ."

The Parkway is a concept of the landscape architect, guided since its inception in 1935 by a sublime document known as the Master Plan. The inherent artistry of the Master Plan is most evident in the realization that the Parkway has no apparent boundary. It is one and the same with the countryside. On farm terrain this effect is achieved by leasing land acquired for the Parkway's wide right-of-way to the Parkway's farmer neighbors.

It is truly a master stroke. Farmers obtain the use of the land and the earnings of its yield in return for a modest fee and proper care. The Parkway benefits from greatly reduced maintenance costs, and the scenic treasure of a natural countryside.

The green and golden harmony we enjoy today, however, was not brought forth without great effort, patience, and skill. It was recognized during the Parkway's early years that the land-lease program should be assigned to a professional agronomist trained in field-crop production and soil management.

The proposed agronomist would meet with the local farmers and persuade them to become partners and caretakers of the thousands of acres of farmland purchased for the transmountain passage of the Parkway.

He would smooth over the resentment of many toward this "mighty particular road" that cleaved their lands in two, even amputating buildings that encroached onto the government side of the boundary line.

He would persuade unpersuaded farmers to accept new farming methods that made proud claims for better yields and soil conservation, and called shame down upon primitive and wasteful ways. He would be a college man entering the homes of the unlettered, asking for a signed contract from men that put their trust in a handshake and the spoken word.

Where could the Parkway find such a man? Such a man was found in Bill Hooper and the finding became one of those rare and cherished events when a man is right for his time and place.

Of course, he had to be a mountain man himself. When he spoke to a Parkway neighbor, he was talking to his own. He knew and respected the innate courtesy and natural manners of the people. He was never in a hurry. He never pressed for a decision. He always accepted an invitation to "come and see me."

Some farmers readily recognized the favorable terms and benefits of a Parkway agreement. For a token fee a man could lease land for crops and pasture. It might not make sense, but he could agree not to grow a "row-crop" like corn or cabbage in successive years. All right, he'd lime and fertilize, and yes, he'd plow on the contour to prevent erosion. He'd even agree to put only one head of cattle or four sheep to the acre on that lush pasture.

And you know, even though Mr. Cooper never said "I told you so," my leased land is looking better than my own land.

Early on, however, there were some mistrustful souls not having any doings with Bill. They'd meet him with a surly eye and say "Git." No hurry. After a while he'd let it be known that he'd be most grateful to meet with Mr. Whomever whenever he'd a mind to. And one day, sure enough. . . .

Bill looks back on those early times with a tinge of regret for their passing. They had a man-to-man directness that gave the feel of trust. But an inevitable affluence came with the increasing productivity of the land, and, increasingly, Bill found himself dealing with attorneys representing the lessee rather than with the lessee himself.

Change is constant, however, and Bill simply applied his practical approach to suit the needs of a more meticulous society. The bottom line is there to see. Today is much improved from yester-year. The mountain farms are greener. The corn is taller, the yield greater. Large firm heads of cabbage are harvested by the truck-load. Cattle fatten knee-deep in pasture. The Parkway visitor sees a verdant, productive farm scene.

Life is an art, not a science, and what greater artist than a practical man with style. Bill Hooper retired from the National Park Service in 1974. He is the recipient of well-deserved awards from the Park Service and from his alma mater, Appalachian State University. He has certain other honors:

> The rustic boundary of the rail fence
> The wind-sheen of sunlight passing over ripening wheat
> The aroma of buckwheat in bloom

> These and all things like them
> Honor the way he touched the land.

Highland Farms

Roanoke to Grandfather Mountain
(121.4 to 291.9 miles)

The Blue Ridge mountains north of Roanoke are a lofty, spur-thrust ridge outlined by parallel lowlands. Between Roanoke and Grandfather they form the high eastern rim of the Blue Ridge plateau.

North of Roanoke, all streams draining the Blue Ridge enter the Atlantic.

Buck Mountain Overlook
123.2 miles
A 30-minute hike leads to the top of Buck Mountain, which provides a panoramic view of Southern Roanoke.

South of Roanoke the Blue Ridge crest line is the drainage divide between the Gulf of Mexico and the Atlantic. Gulf-bound streams flow westerly through broad valleys and interlocking highlands. Streams to the Atlantic cascade down the Blue Ridge escarpment into the Piedmont.

The Parkway roams over the plateau, often skirting the escarpment edge. Panoramas of the Piedmont alternate with closeups of highland farms. The Parkway fits into the farmland scene. Farmer neighbors lease the right-of-way land and till it with their own. Crops grown throughout the countryside are seen along the motor road.

Forests arch the roadway. Oak, hickory, birch, maple, and pine rise above an evergreen understory of rhododendron and mountain laurel. Gray squirrels, foxes, and quail abound. Open areas, lush with grass and clover, are the home of groundhog and cottontail.

The scene is a picture of farming progress: green pastures with herds of stocky Herefords or sleek Guernseys; sheep "fat" with wool; fields of corn, buckwheat, oats, and cabbage; new homes, and fences well tended.

But these themes of the present mingle with the ways of long ago. Nowhere is the old rail fence more apparent than over the open land of the bounding mountainscape. Log cabins, modernized with clapboards and paint, repose snugly in cove and hollow. Even in this era of electricity, the chalky blue smoke of a wood fire wreaths from stone chimneys and the flickering light of a kerosene lamp peers from a window or two. The years have brought comforts more than changes. The quietude of old cabin days rests throughout the green-clad hills.

View of Masons Knob
126.6 miles
elev. 1,425

John Mason settled at the foot of his namesake mountain in 1750, a few years before the French and Indian War. As was common to the time, his sturdy dwelling served as a stockade during the Indian raids. Like the typical frontier dwelling, the walls were probably of heavy logs with small, square peepholes for windows. Windows were not designed for the view, but as a line of sight for putting a bead on the Indian.

Poages Mill
129.3 miles
elev. 2,032

Back Creek threads the valley below where Squire Elijah Poage (1823-1900) operated his saw and grist mill. An enterprising cabinetmaker, Elijah wanted a means to engage his considerable mechanical ability. Accordingly, he applied to the local court in 1848 for a writ of *ad quod dammum* (to that dam). This ancient document called for the sheriff to summon twelve "fit" men to view the proposed dam site and determine any potential harm to the community or obstruction to the passage of fish or navigation.

Back Creek, at the headwaters of the Roanoke River, was about as far back as any fish would want to go. As for navigation, Back Creek probably never saw a row boat. The appointees smiled on Elijah's cause and the court returned a favorable report.

Elijah continually expanded and improved his operation. All mills ground corn, but his mill was the only local means for grinding wheat. He cut timber with a straight saw operating within a frame, or sash. At the first opportunity he replaced this difficult method with the more efficient circular saw, said to be the first in Roanoke County.

Payment for services was often a share of the product. Elijah the cabinetmaker used his share of the lumber to make furniture and coffins. In due time he became the local undertaker.

His community recognized him as a man of stature. He was appointed Justice of the Peace and known ever thereafter as Squire Poage. The mill and the man were one of a kind. When the Squire died the mill lapsed into decline. The mill wheel turned a few more years and then was still.

Lost Mountain Overlook
129.9 miles
elev. 2,200

Whatever the Blue Ridge Parkway may one day become, its genesis belongs to the landscape architect and the road-building engineer. There are many places along the mountain miles where their skill and care is evident. Lost Mountain overlook is a modest, appropriate example:

> We enjoy the quiet, restful view
> So perfectly presented that the art
> of the artist is concealed.
> The island of lyonia shrubs,
> The curving rock wall,
> Inviting you to sit beneath the stretch
> and shade of white pines.
> The evergreen gloss of mountain laurel,
> That just happened to be growing here
> and was invited to stay.

MOUNTAIN LAUREL

America is a resource-conscious society. The scenery so carefully presented here is a resource. Its value must be weighed against the value of commercial development. Can the scenery be lost? No one knows how Lost Mountain got its name.

Slings Gap
133.0 miles
elev. 2,860

How can a name be a shortcut? Why do we say Sam for Samuel, or Hank for Henry? A Mr. Schilling once lived here. In his day and time not many people in the community could read or write. Folks might ask, "What's that feller's name?" but seldom inquired, "How you spell it?" Under such circumstances Schilling became Shuhling, then Sling. Slings Gap is the Parkway portal to the Blue Ridge plateau, a country quilt of pastures and cabbages, wheat, barley, buckwheat and corn. *(Blue Ridge Parkway Superintendent Sam P. Weems, 1954).*

Bull Run Knob Parking Overlook
133.6 miles
elev. 2,890

An incident in the French and Indian War—the time is early October 1756. The first tints of fall color lie subdued beneath an ominous sky. Three horsemen—a leader, a servant, and a guide—approach the Blue Ridge from the western slopes. They pause briefly at the summit, resting their steeds and discussing their descent into the Blackwater Valley.

The guide gestures and describes a route by way of Green Creek, leading through foothills toward the Grassy Hill. "From there we can strike due south and reach Fort Trail." The leader nods. The men remount and pass down the mountain forest.

Colonel George Washington is on an inspection tour of the forts along the frontier from Maryland to Carolina. Times are desperate. Indian raiders stirred by General Braddock's defeat (1755) in Pennsylvania slaughter the isolated settlers and burn their homes.

Washington, commander in chief of the Virginia frontier, calls for the settlers to join his Virginia regulars. Oppressed by fear, distrust, and reluctance to leave their families, frontiersmen are slow to comply.

They serve, when they serve at all, as militiamen for limited periods of duty. At the sound of an Indian war whoop they dash wildly from the source of terror. These are the darkest days of the French and Indian War. If the French possessed an army for occupation, they could gain the entire mountain region. Were the Indians capable of an organized campaign, they could drive the white usurpers from their hunting grounds.

But the French, though victorious in battle, decline to advance in strength beyond their Great Lakes strongholds. The Indians waste their military advantage with victory revels of drunkenness and torture.

Time is on the side of the frontiersmen, time to adjust to this strange wilderness. Time is also an ally of young Colonel Washington, time to recruit, to instill discipline, to build forts.

He leaves headquarters in Winchester and tours the frontier forts. The regulars lack discipline and morale. The militia reluctantly answer the call to defend their communities.

The scene at Fort Vause, near present Shawsville south-west of Roanoke, fits the familiar, sorry pattern. Captain Hog, in charge of the fort, is lax in command. Settlers claim he and his eighteen regulars remain at the fort rather than patrol for hostile Indians. The militia stationed on temporary duty lazily pass their thirty days' service, refus-ing to aid in construction of the still unfinished fort.

The fort is vital. Four months before, a party of French and Indians destroyed the nearby stockade of Ephraim Vause, capturing the handful of defenders. "Why," pon-ders Washington, "do not the settlers strive in their own behalf?"

The Colonel has no troop escort as he leaves Fort Vause for the Blue Ridge—just his guide and a servant. Indian raiders are active. News of their forays jangles the frontier grapevine. A war party lies in ambush along the Colonel's route. Shortly before he approaches, the Indian leader decides to leave his post and instructs his braves to fire only on travelers passing northward. Washington, riding southward, passes unharmed. He completes his tour and returns to Winchester.

The French and Indian War is a contest for possession of North America. The British colonists, east of the mountains, attach little interest to the conflict. The French are no menace, but they are a profitable source of trade. Let the king fight his own battles.

The frontiersmen, moving into the mountains, are not as complacent. They fear the French and their Indian allies. During the 1750s, they are not the deadly fighters history has depicted. For the present, they are recent immigrants in a violent wilderness. They have no love for the English king. Regal tyranny impelled them to leave their homeland. They will fight to save their homes, but not join an English army to march against the French.

By order of necessity they adjust to frontier life. Confi-dence breeds skill and courage. In 1774 Major Andrew Lewis and his mountaineers decisively beat their Indian foes at Point Pleasant in West Virginia.

Men of the same stock become the most dependable of General Washington's command and win honors at Saratoga, Cowpens, and Kings Mountain. The discour-agement that dogs the young colonel in the Indian Wars is the making of him as a general in the Revolution. On the frontier he learns the fundamentals of soldiering—not the exciting, fame-catching glamor of battle, but the prin-ciples of discipline.

Poor Mountain
134.9 miles
elev. 2,975

Poor Mountain, the high point on the left horizon, is named for a Major Poore who served under Andrew Lewis in the French and Indian War, 1754-63.

Settlers came to the Roanoke area in the early 1740s and established themselves without much Indian resist-

ance. But the inevitable conflict between France and
Great Britain for North America led to an Indian assault
on the frontier.

France and Britain each claimed the Ohio Valley. The
native tribes, Shawnee, Mingo, and Delaware, were more
compatible with the French, who preferred trade to col-
onization. The British were land-hungry and came to
America by the boatload.

Armed by the French, Indian war parties annihilated
their foes and panicked thousands, who fled the frontier in
terror from western New York to western Virginia.

George Washington and Andrew Lewis were charged
with the defense of the Virginia frontier. The first retalia-
tion in the winter of 1756 was more vengeful than pru-
dent. Lewis assembled a force of 340 men and about 100
Cherokee allies at Fort Prince George in the Roanoke
Valley near Salem, Va. The frontiersmen were free-
spirited and resented authority. They never reached their
objective, the Indian towns in Ohio. Military discipline
fell victim to harsh winter, lack of food, and uncertainty.
Lewis proceeded to the Ohio River, but chose not to cross
and engage the Indians for lack of confidence in his dis-
pirited men. Many perished making it homeward as best
they could.

But Andrew Lewis and his frontiersmen returned, six
hundred strong, in 1774. They met the attack of Shawnee
chief Cornstalk and his eight hundred warriors at Pt.
Pleasant, on the Ohio River. Losses were heavy on both
sides but the Indians could not prevail. Sullen and
exhausted, they returned to towns already under destruc-
tive attack by a Virginia force under Lord Dunmore. The
Virginia frontier settlements were secure from Indian
raiders.

Adney Gap
136.0 miles
elev. 2,690

"Thomas Adney was born in King's Square, Clerkenwell
Parish, London, England, about 1740 and died about
1805 at Adney Gap, Virginia. He was the first Adney to
reach America, being forcibly taken aboard a ship which
landed him at Charles Town, S.C. in 1760. He resided for
some time at the Quaker settlement on Little River, near
Cape Fear, where he met his future wife, Elizabeth Dunn,
a daughter of Daniel Dunn, a Quaker recently arrived
from Dublin, Ireland. Thomas removed after 1774 to
Franklin County, Virginia. He was trained as a civil
engineer in England, and after coming to America operated a hemp mill at Adney Gap, taught school, surveyed
land and taught his sons to become mill builders and

owners, which occupation they followed in their new
homes in Ohio.

"On 2 April 1798, Thomas purchased from Jacob
Miller a tract of 281 acres of land which was afterward
known as Adney Gap, situated at the summit of the Blue
Ridge. The farm at Adney Gap was never sold. The sons,
John and Daniel, in Ohio, decided that it wasn't worth
their time to go back and settle up the estate." *(John R.
Adney, Genealogist, Miles, Iowa, 1950)*

**The Legend of
Sweet Annie Hollow**
*138.6 miles
elev. 2,889*

Annie, a widow by fate and a friendly sort by nature,
resided in the hollow during the Revolution. Troopers of
the Continental Army were frequent visitors and, repor-
tedly, she entertained them "in a most irreligious manner." Her neighbors took a dim view of the situation and
Annie obliged by leaving the country. But though Annie
didn't live there any more, the troopers landmarked her
homesite as Sweet Annie's Hollow.

**View of
Cahas Knob**
*139.9 miles
elev. 3,015*

Cahas (Kah-Hayes) Knob (elev. 3,560) is a free-standing
mountain rising above the foothills immediately east of
the Blue Ridge plateau. "Cahas" is believed to be
derived from the native Totero Indian word for crow, or
"ka-hi." The Totero, or Tutelo, lived among the foothills
of the Virginia Blue Ridge. Apparently they were a semi-
nomadic people, hunting and farming from their encamp-
ments along the river banks. Numerous Indian relics,
including hoes made from the shoulder blades of deer,
have been unearthed from the fertile bottomlands at the
foot of Cahas Knob.

During the Civil War, Cahas Knob was one of several
hideouts for a small band of desperadoes that terrorized
the local people. Time and again "patteroles," or patrols,
pursued them over the knob and other neighboring mountains. But they managed to escape and continue their
raids, burning property, looting, and "taking the bread
warm from the oven."

Finally a man in Boone's Mill, a town at the foot of the
mountain, caught one of his slaves with a container of
food. Questioned, the slave admitted he knew the whereabouts of the gang and had been feeding them for some
time.

Guided by the unhappy slave, a "patterole" went to the
hideout. The men surrounded the place and carefully hid
themselves. The slave then strode near the hideout and
rapped a stone three times against a large rock. For a tense
moment no sound was heard. Then three sullen men came
into the open and approached the black.

Before they could protect themselves, the riflemen
sprang the trap and the long chase was over. One of the
desperadoes was freed providing he left the country for
life. The other two received the death sentence.

As was the custom of the time, the men were put before a firing squad and shot. Half of the rifles used were loaded with blanks, the other half with live rounds. No one of the executioners knew the contents of his rifle. But one member of the squad claimed for certain that his gun was loaded. ''I bore down on his suspender button and shot it plumb off.''

View of Devil's Backbone
143.9 miles
elev 2,708
Roadside easel: The Drainage Divide

To the mountaineer, geographic features of rocky and rough appearance are commonly prefixed with the word ''devil.'' Devil's Backbone is a sheer, knifelike spur jutting out to the right between the overlook and Pine Spur. A few struggling trees and shrubs maintain a root-hold along the spine of the Devil, but large patches on the steep sides are bare but for a scant cover of lichens and mosses.

Straightaway from the overlook is a long view of the Blackwater Valley. The low, sway-backed ridge on the left is Grassy Hill, hiding the growing town of Rocky Mount. On the left Cahas Knob reaches away from the Parkway and the north tip of the Blue Ridge plateau.

Pine Spur Gap
144.3 miles

For many years the top of the mountain by Pine Spur Gap was the home of a strong, hardworking woman known as Aunt Lizzie Price. Her cabin formerly stood near the present access from the motor road.

Aunt Lizzie was born a slave, below the mountains, in 1845. She gave birth to her first child during the year of the surrender.

Several years later, Aunt Lizzie remarried and came to Pine Spur. Here she and her husband bought a ''boundry'' of farmland and began to make their own way. They lived the hard but ''not without its rewards'' life of the mountain farmer. Then hard times came knocking on Aunt Lizzie's door, taking away her husband and leaving her with a family of eight children.

But she was stout of spirit as well as of body and managed to raise her family ''anyway she could.'' This included running the farm and working for her neighbors, spinning cloth, knitting, sewing, or ''scratchin' around a corn hill.''

Once Aunt Lizzie took a job ''topping'' corn with a crew of men. ''If you can keep up with the men, I'll pay you a man's wages,'' said her employer. She did and earned an eye-popping 50 cents a day.

After her family grew up and she became a little settled with age, Aunt Lizzie liked to light up her pipe and brag about those hardworkin' days. ''I could bind a bundle of oats, give it a heave over my back and tie up another'n afore it hit the ground.''

She had a ''heap of spart'' (spirit) and the spark of life glowed long and brightly—for 108 years.

**View from
Pine Spur**
*144.8 miles
elev. 2,709*

white pine	striped maple	rosebay
flowering	lynn or	rhododendron
dogwood	basswood	mountain
yellow poplar	mountain	winterberry
persimmon	laurel	swamp dogwood

WHITE PINE

The many white pines about the overlook and on the spur stretching down to the foot of the mountains give good reason for the name Pine Spur. From this point southwest to Blowing Rock, N.C., the white pine holds equal sway with the hardwoods and in many sections is the most abundant tree.

It is the tallest pine in the Highlands and one of the loveliest. Mature trees generally exceed a hundred feet, and a few reach a hundred and fifty feet.

In summer the conical profiles of the tulip tree, in the immediate foreground, screen much of the pine growing on the spur. But they do not screen the winsome view of Cahas Knob on the left, and long, low Grassy Hill on the right, with the Blackwater Valley in between.

Bell Spring House
146.6 miles

''The spring was built by my uncle, Riley Poff. I'd guess it to be about 1910. My father bought his place a few years later.

''The spring's a good one. Always cool and fresh. We kept our butter, milk and canned fruit there. Like a refrigerator. Set most things right in the water in a stone jar.

''William Poff, father to the man who built this one, had a spring he was mighty particular about. He'd clean his spring out only by the 'sign.' Had something to do with the moon. He'd get him his almanac and read when was the best time. Then he'd clean and salt it.

''Some things you find in a spring, like spring lizards and crawfish, might bother fussy people, but they don't seem to hurt the water none. I've heard of people telling that a spring lizard meant good water. I had an uncle, Henry McNiel, to swallow one. His spring water came through a pipe and he swallowed it afore he knowed it. That set him a-gaggin' something awful, but his hurt was more'n his head than his stomach.'' *(Moyer Bell, Floyd County, Va., 1952)*

SALAMANDER OR SPRING LIZARD

**Smart View
Overlook into
Pigg River Valley**
*154.1 miles
elev. 2,564*

black locust	red maple	flowering
scarlet oak	sweet birch	dogwood
white oak	pignut hickory	virginia pine
		red cedar

The typical overlook scans a sweep of the countryside. Here the view is guided by two converging slopes. They drop sharply to form a ''gun sight'' aimed into the far beyond. Long cross-rows of lowland hills and valleys gradually dissolve into vagueness and blue mist.

Close by, the oval profiles of flowering dogwood trim a green boundary around the overlook. In May they are completely white with blossoms. In fall the leaves turn red, deepening into purple. And when the leaves are gone, blood-bright berries glisten on the twigs.

The wood of flowering dogwood is durable and close grained. It wears slowly and smoothly and makes the best shuttles for commercial looms. Less than a century ago, hand-powered looms were common in the Southern Highlands. Now their memento is the spindle-shaped shuttle, resting on the mantelpiece.

If the need arises, the twigs make a passable toothbrush. Once the cleaning end is chewed sufficiently, its tough fibers enable a good massage for teeth and gums. The typical use for a toothbrush of this type, however, is to "dip" snuff.

Smart View Recreation Area
154.5 miles
500 acres

FLOWERING DOGWOOD

AZALEA

Picnic grounds; hiking trails; rest rooms; water fountain; Trail cabin exhibit.

Smart View recreation area extends from the Blue Ridge Plateau down to the fringing foothills. The name "Smart" is borrowed from a post office, formerly located nearby, and applies to the scenery. Far reaching, mistily green, and peaceful, it is a "right smart view."

The entrance road curves from the Parkway and heads toward the picnic grounds. Sleepy eyed cattle graze in the bordering pasture. Some wade knee deep into the coolness of a pond spangled with water lilies.

Uphill from the pond and facing the "smart view" itself is the Trail cabin. Built in the early 1890s of rough hewn logs, it is typical of the one room pioneer dwellings of two centuries ago. The cabin was inhabited until 1925, then stripped of floor and loft and used as a barn.

A spring flowing from beneath a nearby yellow poplar supplied water to both man and beast. Just above the spring, Mrs. Trail tended her garden plot. Tucked into the mountain vastness, the Trails lived in comparative solitude. But could anyone ever tire of the view just outside their cabin door?

Smart View Trail encircles the picnic grounds through a composition of forest and field. Along the way are some giant-sized sassafras and redbud, almost overcome with age and grapevines. Rennet Bag Trail is named for the creek that heads in Smart View and flows down mountain to join the Smith River.

In days gone by, folks made cheese by curdling milk in the baglike "true" stomach, or rennet, of a calf. Some one, so the story goes, placed the rennet bag by the stream and it washed on down during a rainstorm.

Just beyond Trail cabin are the picnic tables, set in a forest understory of dogwood. In May they arbor the pathways with white, dense as the leaves to come. Red-bud adds a measure of pink. Soon the pink and the flame azaleas are bedizened with blooms while their leaves are still unfolding. Columbine, trillium, and fire pink cover the ground with vibrance and color. Smart View is right smart the season round, but never lovelier than in spring.

Forest trees and shrubs
Oak and hickory with a dogwood, azalea understory

Locally rare trees

post oak	*red mulberry*	*hackberry*
Fraser magnolia		

Common trees and shrubs

scarlet oak	*shagbark*	*dogwood*
chestnut oak	*sweet, or*	*red bud*
red oak	*black, birch*	*staghorn*
white oak	*red maple*	*sumac*
black oak	*black, or*	*blackhaw*
deerberry or	*sour, gum*	*viburnum*
gooseberry	*sassafras*	*pink azalea*
pignut	*serviceberry*	*flame azalea*

DEER BERRY

Common Flowers

Spring

allegheny	*may apple*	*yellow stargrass*
blackberry	*common*	*blue-eyed*
pink lady's	*cinquefoil*	*grass*
slipper	*fire pink*	*stonecrop*
wild geranium	*columbine*	*field*
casper spurge	*bebb's zizia*	*hawkweed*
solomon's	*crested dwarf*	*small's*
plume	*iris*	*ragwort*
solomon's	*pussy's toes*	*violets*
seal	*four-leaved*	*paniced*
	milkweed	*bellflower*

LADY'S SLIPPER

Summer

rattlesnake	*spotted star*	*smooth*
hawkweed	*thistle*	*gerardia*
yarrow	*Torrey's wild*	*horse nettle*
black	*licorice*	*pokeweed*
snakeroot	*beard tongue*	*touch-me-not*
deptford pink	*alumroot*	*mullein*
purple bluet	*heal-all*	*joe-pye weed*
spotted		*ironweed*
wintergreen		*boneset*

Fall

GOLDFINCH

crown-beard
bull thistle
autumn
  sneezeweed
white wood
  aster

field
  goldenrod
dyer's weed
  goldenrod
wave aster

rough
  goldenrod
silverrod
tall goldenrod

Birds and Other Wildlife

WOOD PEEWEE

RUFFED GROUSE

prairie
  warbler
black-and-white
  warbler
black-throated
  blue warbler
redstart
ovenbird
red-eyed vireo
wood peewee
crested
  flycatcher
chipping
  sparrow
grasshopper
  sparrow

field sparrow
goldfinch
towhee
indigo bunting
cardinal
robin
bluebird
wood thrush
meadowlark
brown
  thrasher
catbird
tufted titmouse
downy
  woodpecker

flicker
black-billed
  cuckoo
yellow-billed
  cuckoo
mourning
  dove
crow
barn swallow
ruby-throated
  hummingbird
ruffed grouse
bobwhite
gray squirrel
cottontail
fence post lizard

Parkway Guide *continues*

FENCE POST LIZARD

**View from
Shortt's Knob**
*157.6 miles
elev. 2,806*

Amos B. Shortt, trapper, lives below the snub-nosed knob
that bears his family name. At one time he maintained
several traplines over the rolling terrain seen from the
overlook and made a fair income from the sale of pelts.
Presently the fur market is down and Amos "don't aim for
nothin' but to pass off the time."

"I been at it for more'n fifty years and used to make out
pretty good. Now there ain't much left around. Only
foxes, possum, and polecat."

Amos lives in a cabin of hewn logs whose antiquity is
concealed beneath clapboards and white paint. His work-
shop is nearby, a red shed filled with pelts and drying-
boards. A litter of traps and carcasses lie outside the door.

"Polecat and possum are awful easy to ketch. They're
dumb as you please. Only have to set the trap and cover it
with leaves. Ketchin' a fox is lots harder but I've got lots
uv'm. A fellow one time asked me how I done so good. I
tole him, 'You fix a trap and go off and come back. If you
cain't tell where its at, you'll ketch a fox. We got both
kinds, the red and the gray. One's just as sharp as the
other.'"

RED FOX

GRAY FOX

Tramping the countryside, out on his trapline, Amos
takes a bag, a cane, and a .22 revolver. The cane is a
straight four-foot staff used with numbing effect on the
skulls of his catch. Only when absolutely necessary will
he shoot an animal. A bullet may damage the pelt.

Each time Amos traps a skunk, an ill-smelling duel
ensues. "The polecat dreads the smell of scent bad as a
human does. He don't throw his scent till you hit'm." If
Amos scores squarely with his "skunk knocker," the
"big stink" may be prevented. Otherwise the results are
bound to be aired about. *(1952)*

Rakes Mill Pond
*162.4 miles
elev. 2,477*

A hundred years or so ago, people who came to Jarmon
Rakes's mill pond had the pleasure of fishing for trout
while they waited for their "turn of meal." The lucky
fisherman took home his string of speckled beauties and
had a feed of fresh trout fried in corn meal. *(Guy Dillon,
1948)*

Tuggle's Gap
*165.3 miles
elev. 2,752*

*Floyd, 6 miles north; Stuart, 21 miles south; 24 miles
south and east to Fairy Stone State Park; swimming;
fishing; boating; camping; and picnicking.*

Sometime before the Revolutionary War a Reverend
Mr. Tuggle came up the Smith River Valley from the east
and settled at the foot of the Blue Ridge. The crossing
over the mountains above his home became known as
Tuggle's Gap.

One winter, shortly after the Civil War, and years after
the Reverend Mr. Tuggle passed on to his reward, a
bedraggled soldier came to a farm below Tuggle's Gap
and asked the people for some food. They willingly fed

him and invited him to "stay the night." The soldier thanked them but thought he had best get over the mountains. A storm was threatening and he wanted to reach his destination as soon as possible. He waved them his thanks and trudged up toward Tuggle's Gap.

The "grape vine" soon informed the local people that a stranger was passing through. They watched, but never saw him and finally his disappearance ceased to interest them.

But the following spring a resident of the gap happened to see a pair of legs sticking out from a hollow log. Upon investigating he discovered the corpse of the unknown soldier.

A group of neighbors took it upon themselves to give him a proper burial. They cut a six-foot section of the hollow log and boarded up the ends, with the corpse secured inside. The soldier was buried nearby in the grave of the unknown soldier of Tuggle's Gap.

STRIPED SKUNK

**Rocky Knob
Recreation Area**
167-169 miles
4,130 acres

Naturalist program; campfire talks; guided hikes; trails; picnic grounds; campgrounds; water fountains; rest rooms; housekeeping cabins.

The terrain of Rocky Knob Recreation Area is dominated by its namesake mountain, (elev. 3,572). The knob rises from the plateau like the rounding crest of a wave, then sweeps downward into the easterly lowlands.

On its northern flank, the mountain is covered with blue grass and redtop. Livestock graze and fatten. Their salt block is beneath a group of roadside oaks and hickories. Here they gather in the shade and watch the cars go by.

Rail fences border the way. Separate spur roads lead to a campgrounds and a picnic area. The campgrounds contain a vigorous growth of Chinese chestnuts planted by the Park Service in 1952 in cooperation with the U.S. Forest Service (USFS). In general, the Chinese chestnut is planted in orchard fashion for nut production. Here they are planted in a tight stand to see how they develop and shape themselves untended in the habitat once dominated by the native chestnut.

The trees are taller than those of an orchard, but not sufficient for timber production. They produce a fair nut crop but far short of the prodigious autumn harvests that once lay in the open burrs of the American chestnut.

ROSEBAY RHODODENDRON

Will that day ever return? The amazing tenacity of the chestnut sprouts rising from the bases of trees killed by the blight, keep the hope alive. The USFS's continuing efforts to produce blight-resistant strains and hybrids may one day bear chestnuts.

The picnic grounds are set in a cool evergreen bower of winterberry, rosebay rhododendron, and hemlock. Each picnic site is a nook of sylvan solitude. A portion of the picnic grounds has an area for group parking near an open

EASTERN OR CANADIAN HEMLOCK

field. It lends itself to family reunions where the generations blend together as they play games, munch fried chicken, and listen to the grandparents tell the sagas of their kin.

Forest Trees and Shrubs

Picnic and campgrounds
An eastern hemlock-mixed hardwoods association, rosebay rhododendron-mountain winterberry understory.

eastern hemlock	yellow poplar	black locust
white oak	white ash	flowering crab
red oak	black cherry	white pine
chestnut oak	red maple	yellow birch
rosebay rhododendron	serviceberry	flame azalea
mountain winterberry	mountain laurel	deerberry
	staghorn sumac	minniebush
	sassafras	American elder

Common Flowers

Spring

early saxifrage	large flowered trillium	mouse-ear hawkweed
chickweed	solomon's seal	small's ragwort
buttercup	speckled wood lily	dewberry
common cinquefoil	wild geranium	blackberry
pussy's toes	fire pink	field hawkweed
bebb's zizia	bowman's root	
golden alexander		

Summer

purple bluet	black snakeroot, or cohosh	whorled loosestrife
beard tongue	smooth gerardia	small-flowered bunchflower
rattlesnake plaintain	pale touch-me-not	spotted star thistle
rattlesnake hawkweed	heal-all	mullein
panicled bellflower	panicled hawkweed	black-eyed susan
alumroot		yarrow
mullein		wild hydrangea

MOUNTAIN HOLLY OR WINTERBERRY

Fall

white wood aster	dyer's-weed goldenrod	white snakeroot
wave aster	tall goldenrod	tall white lettuce
Curtis goldenrod	silverrod	bull thistle
	ladies' tresses	bottle gentian

Common Ferns

Cinnamon   Christmas   marginal
polypody   rattlesnake   shield
   ebony spleenwort

REDSTART

Birds and Other Common Wildlife

bluejay   field sparrow   chimney swift
crow   song sparrow   tufted titmouse
Carolina wren   red-eyed vireo   ruby-throated
catbird   hummingbird
brown   hooded   downy
   thrasher   warbler   woodpecker
meadowlark   black-throated   flicker
robin   blue warbler   white-breasted
wood thrush   chestnut-sided   nuthatch
wood pewee   warbler   mourning
phoebe   black-and-white   dove
crested   warbler   ruffed grouse
   flycatcher   southern   bobwhite
goldfinch   parula   red-tailed
towhee   warbler   hawk
indigo bunting   ovenbird   turkey vulture
chipping   yellow-breasted   gray squirrel
   sparrow   chat   chipmunk
     redstart   groundhog

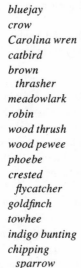

CHESTNUT-SIDED WARBLER

HOODED WARBLER

Parkway Guide *continues*

COTTONTAIL

View from the Saddle

168.0 miles
elev 3,380

The Saddle is a swaybacked ridge connecting two high points on Rocky Knob Mountain (elev 3,572). Forming a portion of the Blue Ridge crest line, the Saddle provides a broad view of the Blue Ridge. Left, the plateau rolls northwestward. In front is the bounding outline of the Blue Ridge crest, divide between the Gulf of Mexico and the Atlantic. Right, the escarpment lunges steeply into the Piedmont lowlands.

On the opposite side of the view, looking across the plateau, Buffalo Mountain humps into the horizon like a charging bull buffalo.

Below the Saddle, in the hollow, is the former dwelling of James Monroe Compton, built in 1902. Much of this land, including the steep slopes of Rocky Knob, was farmed. Now the fields are covered with a new forest of Virginia pine, sweet birch, and yellow poplar that have taken the place of the chestnut "orchards" every mountain farmer prized and kept.

In the mid-1920s the American chestnut was practically exterminated by a blight. Largely because of its bountiful nut crop, it was the most valuable tree of the forest. Entire families earned enough in trade to keep themselves in clothes and shoes. Man, wife, and young'uns gathered the nuts into bags and baskets and hauled them to nearby merchants. Often a man on horseback rode through the country spreading the word that the country merchant was ready to buy. The price varied from three to twelve cents a pound. Enough remained on the ground to feed the domesticated turkeys and razor-back hogs that roamed the forest.

Chestnut wood, because of its durability and the ease with which it may be split, made the best fence rails. Nearly all the rail fences seen today in these mountains are of chestnut.

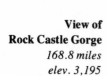

CHESTNUT

View of Rock Castle Gorge

168.8 miles
elev. 3,195

Rock Castle Gorge lies steeply below, "boundried" on the far side by the long reach of Brammer Spur. An old mountain road, now used as a hiker's trail, wends five miles down the gorge alongside Rock Castle Creek. The creek is an ebullient freshet, gathering tributaries from each hollow it passes. Up several of the hollows are outcrops of crystalline quartz. Individual crystals are shaped like the hexagonal turrets of a medieval castle. These are the "rock castles" of Rock Castle Gorge.

Prior to 1935, and since the late eighteenth century, the gorge contained the mountain community of Rock Castle. A dozen or so families farmed the slopes and hollows. In 1935 the Federal Resettlement Administration acquired the lands for the National Park Service and public recreation.

The former landowners were reprieved from farming the reluctant soil. They moved away and Rock Castle Gorge returned to its own designs.

The Fins
168-169 miles

Locally, fin-shaped projections of rock poke up above the ground. The rocks of the Blue Ridge plateau have been tilted in the process of subterranean movement geological eons ago. Here the sharply tilted rock occurs in layers of varying resistance to the erosive effects of rain and wind. The "fins" are the handiwork of differential erosion.

Rocky Knob Housekeeping Cabins
174.1 miles

One mile east on Spur Road. Rental information at Rocky Knob (167.1 miles), or Mabry Mill, (176.2 miles).

The cabins were built by the young men of the Civilian Conservation Corps (CCC). The CCC was a nationwide youth program born in 1933 during the Great Depression and phased out in 1942 with World War II. At its peak, over 500,000 young men, ages 17 to 24, worked on government projects in flood control, reforestation, and recreation. The corps offered young men career training and bed and board during a time of massive unemployment and little opportunity.

Several CCC camps were located along the Parkway where youthful energies were guided by Parkway architects and engineers: re-covering the scars of road building with native plants, fighting forest fires, constructing picnic and campgrounds and utility buildings, and laying out the wonderful miles of foot trails that companion the motor road.

Moonshine Still Exhibit at Mabry Mill
176.2 miles

Almost every hollow on the rugged slopes of the Blue Ridge has known, at one time or another, the secret rites for "making a run of licker." Moonshining is a simple and efficient process. Alcohol is distilled from a mash of fermented grain or fruit. Sugar, added to the mash, speeds the fermenting process. The mash is boiled in a copper drum from which vapors pass off through a coiled tube called the worm. The worm sits in a tub of cold running water troughed from a nearby stream. Cooling liquefies the vapor and it collects, drip by drip, in a "singlin' " keg. The singlin's are then poured back into the still, after removal of the mash, and redistilled into "doublin's."

The practiced moonshiner tests the "proof" of his mountain dew by pouring a sample in a Mason jar and shaking it. The more bubbles rising to the top, the stronger the liquor. Enough water is added to save the throat from blistering and then it is ready, for better or worse.

But where are the stills of yesteryear? Moonshining has been a father-to-son tradition. When money was short, making a run of "licker" was a means of cash. Sure, stilling was illegal, but the stills were in the mountains long before the law against it was put on the books. Your neighbor never looked down on you for stillin', sippin', or sellin' white lightning. He was probably doing it himself.

The sons are not following the way of their fathers. Simply put, there are easier ways to make a buck.

Mabry Mill
176.2 miles
elev. 2,855

Coffee shop; souvenir shop; self-guiding trail; gristmill; blacksmith shop; pioneer exhibits.

Built and operated from 1910 to 1935 by E. B. Mabry, this gristmill, sawmill, and the nearby blacksmith shop illustrate the fact that well into the twentieth century mountain communities often depended upon one man's ingenuity to create machinery needed to produce many of the necessities of life.

A self-guiding trail illustrates pioneer mountain industry including a sorghum mill and evaporating pan, soap-making kettle, and old-timey whiskey still. During summer a miller grinds corn and buckwheat, a blacksmith hammers out iron tools and other objects, and a ranger-historian explains the pioneer mountain culture to visitors to the area. On weekends in October demonstrations of sorghum and apple butter making are conducted along the trail, done in the mountain way by mountain people.

The gray and mossy look of Mabry Mill belongs to that of pictures seen in great-grandmother's stereoscope. But the mill doesn't live in the past. It takes you there. A liveliness and sparkle ride in the water tumbling into the water buckets and turning the waterwheel. Perpetually it rumbles and turns.

Inside the building, power pulleys on the drive shaft turn in readiness to take on the belt and work the gristmill. The sweet mustiness of cornmeal lingers by the gristmill. Maybe Uncle Ed Mabry, owner and operator, is only away for lunch and will be back in an hour.

Ed began building his one-man industrial plant in the early 1900s. He and his wife, Lizzie, were thrifty people and saved enough from his pay in the West Virginia coal fields to return home and buy a farm.

However, it was never Ed's intention to make a living behind the plow. Machines, not farm chores, were his natural bent. First he built his blacksmith shop, and closely thereafter, the major portion of the mill. By 1908 he had earned a local reputation as a "man who could fix most anything." Worn-out tools, broken wagons, horses to be shod—he could fix them all.

The mill was kept busy. The farmer's boy came riding the old mare packing a bag of corn. Uncle Ed stood by the gristmill and controlled the grinding while his customer poured the grain. The charge was one-tenth of the meal, and the remainder filled the bag.

Other times a man wagoned in logs to be sawed. This was a worrisome task. The saw required more power than the water supply could maintain. So Uncle Ed had to saw awhile, then wait awhile.

By 1910, Mabry completed his mill with the addition of the front portion, containing a jigsaw and a jointer. His lifelong friend and neighbor, Newton Hylton, admiringly referred to the jigsaw as "a grand invention." Its twin blades cut out wooden rims for wagon wheels, any size, any width. The jointer tongue-and-grooved board lumber from the sawmill.

Up until 1925 Uncle Ed lived a busy and relatively prosperous life. Then things began to go badly for him. The water supply, never overly plentiful, became insufficient for the amount of work to be done. Added to this misfortune, a lame back prevented him from keeping up necessary repairs.

Uncle Ed gradually retired from his enterprises. But Aunt Lizzie took over a share of them, and very capably. Some folks say she turned a better grist than her husband.

Ed Mabry died in 1936 and Aunt Lizzie passed on a few years later. Since 1950 the mill has been operated by National Park Concessions.

A Day with Uncle Newt in the Summer of '56

Out in the blacksmith shop, busy pumping the hand bellows, "puttin' the fire" to his forge, is Uncle Ed's old chum, Newton Hylton. At age 84, Uncle Newton works in the shop eight hours every day except Monday. Cars make him "seasick," so he walks six miles to and from work. Visit with him and he'll pause from his work with the hammer and tongs and offer a comment or two.

Making some horseshoes, he remarks, "These here shoes won't never see a horse, I don't reckon. The ladies use'm to hang behind doors. Menfolks use'm for pitchin' horseshoes." And then in a tone that means both modesty and pride he'll say, "I can't get along like a young feller, but I don't slight my work none." Then his hammer will strike the glowing iron in just the right way and in just the right place.

Old soldiers, and old mountaineers as well, eventually fade away. Mr. Hylton, whose tart humor and generous goodwill is embodied in our "Uncle Newt," passed on to his reward in 1958.

The present blacksmith is Phipps "Festus" Bourne of Elk Creek, Virginia. He has worked the hand bellows and hammered glowing iron into useful forms at Mabry Mill since 1968. Festus makes horseshoes, door knockers, hinges, pot hooks; and fire sets, shovels, poker, and tongs. He is also a pretty good hand at wood carving. Stop by and say hello.

Meadows of Dan, Virginia
177.7 miles
elev. 2,960

U.S. 58, Stuart, Va., 16 miles southeast · Hillsville 21 miles west.

Meadows of Dan is a highlands farm community set within a green ramble of grasslands. Its name is one of many derived from the Old Testament (Joshua 20:47-49).

Not far south of the meadows, the Blue Ridge plateau

comes to an abrupt end in a river-carved labyrinth known as the "Bent." Through it the Dan River twists in ceaseless endeavor to engineer a canyon into the resistant rocks. At one place the Dan almost encircles a giant monolith rising abruptly upward to an uneven pair of pinnacles. These are the Pinnacles of Dan, sheer and jagged as a miniature Matterhorn.

Mayberry Gap Road
180.5 miles
Va. Rt. 634
A line on the "Underground Railway"

The "underground railway" is clouded with misconceptions. Popularly it is thought of as having been a highly organized system for secreting slaves out of the South. Agents, way-stations, and synchronized planning reputedly aided the fugitives.

Actually the underground was mainly a furtive and unplanned exodus of runaway slaves. Singly or in small groups they headed north, often aided by nothing more than the North Star. In some localities they were helped by sympathizers, but very few received aid and guidance over the entire trip.

What organization did exist was largely due to Quakers. The Friends were opposed to slavery on religious principle and generally did what they could to help the fugitives escape.

A route for slaves traveling on foot crossed the Blue Ridge crest at Mayberry Gap, about two road miles west from this point.

View from Groundhog Mountain
188.8 miles
elev 3,030

Observation tower; picnic tables; rest rooms; rail-fence exhibit.

Of all the mammals seen by Parkway visitors, the groundhog arouses the most curiosity. Squat and plump, he busily feeds and noses among the thick, green cover of the roadside. Should an auto pass by, bolt upright he stands on his haunches. Then, for safety's sake, he'll waddle-gallop to his burrow. Other times he barely bothers to stop stuffing himself. "The clover's too good, and I'm getting used to autos. They pass by and never pay me no mind." But the people in the auto do. Many wonder what odd type of creature that could have been.

Groundhogs are now common in the mountains. Farming opened up the highlands and gave them more and better living space. Formerly they were an animal of the forest and fewer in number. The south slopes of Groundhog Mountain were cleared of forest long ago and provided a favored habitat for the plump rodent.

GROUNDHOG

Atop the dome of Groundhog Mountain stands an observation tower. During World War II it was used by the Virginia Forest service. The 3015 view of plateau and piedmont shows it served its purpose well. An interesting feature of the tower is its architecture, derived from that of a tobacco barn.

SNAKE RAIL

BUCK RAIL

POST AND RAIL

The grounds immediately surrounding the tower are bordered by a rail fence exhibit. Three types of field fences are shown: the snake, buck, and post-and-rail. The snake fence, recognized by its zigzag arrangement, is easiest to build but requires the most rails. A pair of cross stakes are often propped against the rails at the interlock to make them withstand the wind. Blocks of stone or wood are frequently placed beneath the bottom rails to preserve them from ground rot.

The buck fence, least common of all rail fences, is seldom seen today. It was used on land too rough and uneven to build any other. The buck fence is named for its resemblance to the sawbuck, a rack with X-shaped ends on which wood is laid for sawing by hand.

The most practical of the old-style rail fences is the post-and-rail, or stake-and-rail. It requires the least material and makes a good, steady fence that doesn't blow down.

The exhibit also includes a section of picket fence, used to enclose the garden and keep livestock and poultry away from the house. "The pickets are sharp so the chickens won't roost on them, and also as a place for Mason jars to dry prior to canning fruits and vegetables. There's little in this world that happens by accident." *(Harley E. Jolley, 1980)*

Pilot Mountain Overlook
189.1 miles
elev. 2,950

Many mountains exceed the Pilot in elevation, but none is more distinctive. Its peculiar outline is etched from an outcrop of quartzite, one of the most durable rocks known. Weathering through millions of years has worn away the softer rocks and carved out the Pilot, (elev. 2,700).

Its profile imaginatively creates a variety of images. It is a castle fortress with high, unscalable walls. It is the form of a body lying in state. It is a distant island, rising above a sea of mist.

The Indian, unlike the white man, was not inclined to name every hill and brook. He gave names only to the outstanding or unusual. To him the Pilot was the Great Guide.

To the first white settlers, who knew it as the Ararat, the mountain may have reminded them of the biblical Ark and the Mount Ararat mentioned in Genesis where the Ark landed after the flood.

Aunt Orelena Puckett Cabin Exhibit
189.9 miles
elev. 2,848

Some people who do great deeds are remembered with monuments. Aunt Orelena Puckett's great deeds were giving kindness and help by the brimming cupful. Her monument is the cabin on Groundhog Mountain.

Aunt Orelena is credited with bringing over a thousand mountaineer babies into the world. She went whenever and wherever called, sometimes on foot, sometimes by horse.

Groundhog Mountain Fences

Her friends tell of a time when the weather was "so rough and slick a body couldn't keep to his feet," but Aunt Orelena pounded nails through the soles of her shoes and made her way to the expectant mother.

She used no medicine—just plenty of soap and water, plus a nip of whiskey flavored with camphor. Folks claim she never lost a child or mother through any fault of her own. People from more than a hundred miles away came to get her to "tend to the bornin'," and remain with the child and mother a few days. Sometimes business was so good that several weeks elapsed before she returned.

These trips were the delight of her life. She liked to tell about them to her friends at home. Her original charge for services about 1890 was $1. It increased to $6 "when times was good." People usually gave her things to eat and use, and this pleased her into all kinds of smiles. She, in turn, goodheartedly gave away many of her gifts to those in need about her.

Folks say that Aunt Orelena was born at the foot of the Blue Ridge in Carroll County. Just when, no one agrees, although her gravestone is probably near right with 1839. To the oldtime mountaineer such things as birthdates "don't make no matter mind." She did recall being married at 16, and June as the month of her birth. "The forest was green when I was a-born and I'm green yet."

She and husband John settled in the foothills below Groundhog Mountain. Here they lived and farmed for almost 20 years. Then in 1874 John bought land up on the mountain and built the small, one-room cabin now so familiar to Parkway visitors. Soon thereafter he made a larger home, but the cabin was lived in off and on. John died in 1912. His wife survived him for many years, a busy midwife. Her last attendance was for her own grand-grandnephew, Maxwell Dale Hawks, in 1939. She died the same year.

Aunt Orelena's unselfishness and willingness to face hardships for others stands as truly remarkable when we learn the tragic story of her motherhood. Of her own twenty-four children, none lived beyond infancy. The eldest, Caroline, died at two years, six months, and four days. When Aunt Orelena gave birth to a child people would say, "You better go see Aunt Orelena's baby now if you want to see it a-livin'."

In her own words she often wished "the bird (stork) would fly by my door." Most people would have become embittered, but Aunt Orelena, bereft of her family and past fifty, began a career of service to her people that lasted almost fifty more.

Her neighbor, Robert Martin, knew her well. "She brung in eight of my ten children. People would just as soon have her as a doctor. She seemed to know what she was about. There wasn't a doctor around no way nearer than Hillsville or Mt. Airy. If anything was a-goin' wrong, she could tell it, and made certain to get a doctor.

"I don't know about her own children. Most of'm didn't likely come to time.

"She had one eye crossed. She warn't a pretty woman, but she was a good'un."

Bluemont Church
191.9 miles

According to Christian beliefs, there is some good in everything. But if ever there was an exception, according to the mountain farmer, it would be the "cussed" rocks strewn over his land. They turn his plow and lame his stock. The backbreaking task of carting them away never ends. They seem to multiply.

When Preacher Bob Childress suggested to his congregation that they build a church from these same bedeviling rocks, all was not harmony in the meeting house. But Preacher Bob persuaded them that the rocks were fine for the purpose. Like faith in God, they would endure forever.

Once the members were convinced, they went willingly to work. Each contributed his or her share of labor and materials. The task was hard and often discouraging, but they had a leader who believed in finishing anything he started.

Bob Childress, by his own admission, had been a rough fellow who packed a gun and did his share of "stillin.'" Law and order were two words he didn't much abide by. But one day Bob became acquainted with a Quaker mission below the Blue Ridge. The gentle wisdom of the Friends made him resolve to change his ways and help others change theirs. He decided to become a Presbyterian minister.

It was not an easy choice for a man of thirty-two with a wife and family. However, they all meant to see it through, and did.

After receiving his degree, Bob returned home to the mountains, working tirelessly to enrich his people with faith in God. A modern circuit rider, he commuted to his several churches by station wagon and traveled as much as a hundred and seventy-six thousand miles in one year. His circuit included four other churches like Bluemont, staunch stone temples of worship.

The Reverend Bob was mighty proud to have been a neighbor and friend of another firm believer in the Good Book, Aunt Orelena Puckett. It didn't "make no matter mind" between them that she was a hardshell Baptist and he a Presbyterian.

Heads were bowed in the stone churches when the reverend died. His son preached his funeral and took his father's place at the pulpits.

Volunteer Gap
193.2 miles
elev. 2,706

The Blue Ridge Crossing of the "Volunteer Road".

"When my granddaddy (1803-1882) come here from Henry County, below the mountain, people had no get-out way to the county seat at Hillsville. They all volunteered and made them a road afore it was ever put on the County." *(Robert Lee Martin, 1952)*

Orchard Gap
193.7 miles
elev. 2,675

APPLE BLOSSOM

Apples prosper on the cool, well-drained slopes of the escarpment. The peculiar fact that large areas are locally free of killing frosts favors a mass of blossoms. Tended by the honey bee and nourished by ample sun and rain, the trees repeat with bumper crops, year after year.

In the early 1900s, Ralph Levering, a Quaker from Tennessee, came to the community and noted the possibilities for apple farming. Though a few small orchards existed, much of the land lay idle. He bought a sizeable tract on the lower slopes and then, with the aid of numerous government pamphlets, assumed the life of a scientific orchardist. He learned of sprays, fertilizers, pruning techniques, and insect pests. And since he also relied on plenty of hard work, the orchard produced handsomely. Now as then, the trees blossom pink each May and bend with juicy fruit each fall.

Wards Gap
195.5 miles
elev. 2,750

There are several ways by which a pioneer acquired land in the mountain region. Some "took up land" by the "cabin right." The new owner had to build a cabin and raise a crop of corn or grain. This entitled him to several hundred acres.

Some received grants of land for military service. Others purchased land from speculators who had acquired huge tracts from the government. However land was obtained, all types of ownership required legal recognition, evidenced by a written document or warrant.

And then there were fellows like Mr. Ward who just came to a place and decided to stay. Squatters had no deed or bill of sale. Mr. Ward probably never gave it a thought. During his time, the late 1700s, who would bother about a rough piece of mountain land?

In fairness to the unknown Mr. Ward, it must be admitted that he may very well have paid for his land in good, hard cash. But like many others of his day, he never bothered to record it in the courthouse.

Fancy Gap
199.4 miles
elev. 2,925

U.S. 52; Hillsville 8 miles north; Mt. Airy 14 miles south.

In the 1830s, travel between Blue Ridge communities and those of the piedmont was a difficult undertaking. The steep escarpment made the descent treacherous and the return an exhausting effort. Too often a stagecoach or freight wagon careened out of control on the downward curves. The upward journey wearied both animals and drivers. In spite of frequent rests, horses and oxen were foam-flecked by the time they reached the summit.

But for the escarpment barrier, a thriving trade would have existed between plateau and piedmont from the start.

Every teamster making the mountain haul was aware of this. But how to make a better road?

One of the teamsters was fourteen-year-old Ira Coltrane, working with a train of freighters. Young Coltrane had many opportunities to ponder the near futility of the mountain haul. On the up-mountain trip, all the teams were hitched to one wagon. After each ascent they returned for the others, one by one.

The trip with loaded wagon going down mountain required skill and caution. Drivers braked their wheels with heavy chains and slid the wagons most of the way.

The road Ira and his fellow teamsters took was known as the Good Spur. It followed the crest of a "good spur" for a road, up to the Blue Ridge crest. Though fairly direct, the grade was uneven and steep.

Beneath the eastern slope of Good Spur stretched a deep valley leading upward to an old mountain crossing. From his wagon seat Ira carefully studied the passage below and in his mind's eye visualized a smoother route.

People have a way of ignoring the inventiveness of fourteen-year-olds. His buddies probably laughed at him and said a man might as well wish for wings. But Ira never gave up his idea. Years later he became Col. Ira B. Coltrane, a member of the North Carolina General Assembly. He convinced this body that such a road was a much needed improvement. The assembly put the colonel in charge and he located a new turnpike across the mountains at a place he named Fancy Gap.

Today, motor cars follow the route Colonel Coltrane laid out in 1853. Today's travel got a big boost from the foresight of a teenage teamster.

The Story of a Courthouse and the Eyes of a Statue

Hillsville, Va., lies 8 miles north on U.S. 52. It is the county seat of Carroll County, a pleasant land whose economic life is in harmony with its resources. The rolling uplands are put to optimum use growing pasture, hay, and corn for beef and dairy herds. The steep, well-drained slopes along its eastern borders are a green array of apple orchards. Fast-growing forests, dominated by white pine, complement the local furniture industry.

Hillsville, in common with the other municipalities in the region, is growth oriented and offers a willing hand to welcome new industry and tourism. The courthouse is the frequent host for recording current business ventures.

Visitors, as well as local residents, pass beneath the gaze of a Confederate soldier, standing stoically on his pedestal. This veteran in gray is the witness of another much less peaceful time, a time when Carroll County Courthouse was the scene of violence and tragedy.

On March 14, 1912, guns spoke in response to a verdict of guilty rendered to Floyd Allen by a jury of his peers. Floyd and five of his kin shot it out with officials of the court. The room became a panic of people fleeing to the doors and dropping from second-story windows. Spurts of flame shot from gun muzzles. Victims screamed and groaned as bullets thudded into their bodies. Black, choking smoke hazed the room and stung the eyes.

The fusillade stopped. The antagonists scattered, leaving the courtroom to the dead and dying.

Never again would the presiding judge call his court to order, or the commonwealth attorney try another case, or the sheriff order his deputies to serve a warrant. One juror and one witness would never again serve the law or any other earthly interest.

All of the Allen group engaged in the firefight fled the scene largely unscathed excepting a sorely wounded Floyd Allen. Slowly, painfully, he walked to his horse and attempted to mount. He fell heavily to the ground. His son, Victor, who was an unarmed spectator at the scene, remained and assisted him to a local hotel and there they spent the night.

Who was Floyd Allen? The nation's press called Floyd the leader of the Allen clan, a fierce group of mountaineers who shot up the court in defiance of law and order.

This was far from the truth, and the truth compounded the tragedy.

Floyd Allen was himself an officer of the law. He served in the capacity of constable or deputy, obtaining these positions either by judicial appointment or by winning at the polls. He was a successful storekeeper and lived in a fine home fourteen miles from Hillsville on present U.S. 52 at the foot of the Blue Ridge.

Folks described him as handsome, of medium height and build, polite and loyal to those he considered his friends, but possessed of a temper that often sought a violent means to solve a problem.

He was one of a family of ten sired by Jesse Allen, a Confederate soldier who fought and survived four years in service to the Southern cause.

The Allens, like most families, had their occasional differences, but they stuck by each other when trouble came. Trouble came to Floyd Allen and hit him where he was most vulnerable, in defense of his family.

Violence was a specter that rode shotgun with Floyd Allen. He resorted to violence on one fateful occasion with a man who later became commonwealth attorney of Carroll County.

And trouble came to Floyd Allen. Floyd had two grown nephews, Wesley and Sidna Edwards, sons of his widowed sister. One Saturday night in the spring of 1911, Wesley exchanged angry words with another young man.

No blows were struck, but tempers simmered. The following Sunday, Wesley and Sidna gathered with fellow Primitive Baptists in a little schoolhouse at Fancy Gap to sing hymns and listen to a preaching by their uncle, the Reverend Garland Allen.

A young man came to the church door and gestured to Wesley. Come on out. Wesley left. When he did not return promptly, Sidna also left and saw his brother set upon by his foe of the previous night, aided by a couple of allies. Sidna joined the fray and the interlopers were driven away.

The episode came to the attention of the courthouse. Indictments were issued against the nephews for fighting and disturbing a religious worship. Indictments were also issued against their foes, but were never brought to court.

The young men came to their Uncle Floyd for advice. "What should we do?"

"This isn't your fight. They are doing this to get at me. Go across the state line and lay low. I'll go to the courthouse and arrange for a hearing."

The young men got jobs in nearby Mt. Airy, N.C., and waited for word from Uncle Floyd.

Meanwhile, the courthouse learned of their whereabouts. Two deputies crossed the state line and loaded them, tied and manacled, on a horse and buggy and headed for the Hillsville jail. The deputies could have chosen a route other than the way by Floyd Allen's house, but that's the way they came. "Let him try something if he dares."

Fourteen miles from Hillsville, the wary deputies and their reluctant passengers passed the home and store of Floyd Allen. Silence. No sound or action disturbed their passage. But not for long. Floyd Allen was en route from Hillsville where he had contracted with the state attorney's office to deliver his nephews. He met the officers near Fancy Gap as they approached the palatial home of his brother, Sidna.

Floyd glared in rising anger as he beheld his nephews tied and trussed like hogs. "You might do that to known criminals, but not to two youths charged with a misdemeanor. Untie them and let them ride into town like men. I give you my word they won't try to escape."

The deputies refused. One pulled his gun and leveled it at Floyd. Floyd snatched it from him and beat it to pieces on a rock. The deputies declined to deliver the prisoners any farther and left the scene. Floyd later surrendered his nephews to the court. They were tried and convicted, Wesley for sixty days; Sidna for thirty days.

They were present and participants at the courthouse shootout, March 14, 1912. Also present and armed were Floyd's son, Claude; his brother, Sidna, and a nephew, Friel Allen. Unknown to his defense attorneys, Floyd Allen had a gun.

As though prepared for a shoot-out, the commonwealth

attorney and the chief clerk were armed. This was a violation of court rules that also applied to the Allens. Only the sheriff and his deputies could legally possess firearms.

The evidence had been presented on the previous day. The judge, aware that trouble might occur, held court an hour early at 8:00 A.M. But three hundred people crowded in to hear the verdict.

Floyd was convicted of interfering with law officers in performance of their duties and sentenced to a year in prison. A deputy came forward to conduct him to a jail cell. Floyd Allen looked steely-eyed at his oppressors. The commonwealth attorney and the chief clerk gripped their hand guns. Floyd reached inside his coat. Did he have a gun?

"Gentlemen, I'm not going."

No one knows who fired the first shot, but everyone agrees it wasn't Floyd. He fell, shot in the leg, across the cowering and prostrate form of one of his attorneys. "Get away from me. They'll kill me shooting at you." Floyd arose and vaulted the railing extending below the judge's bench and drew his gun, firing at his enemies.

The Allens' war was against the commonwealth attorney and the chief clerk and anyone else firing at them. They claimed no malice or intent to harm the judge, the juror, or the witness. They were unfortunate victims of the fray.

Retribution came swiftly. Floyd surrendered without resistance in his hotel room. His son Claude and nephews Sidna Edwards and Friel Allen surrendered or were captured soon thereafter. His brother Sidna and nephew Wesley Edwards hid out in the surrounding hills for a few weeks, easily evading a wary and not too diligent hunting party, and then escaped west where they lived and worked in Des Moines, Iowa, for several months. Wesley informed his hometown sweetheart of his whereabouts and she led police to their rooming house and peaceful capture.

The trial of Floyd Allen, charged with slaying the commonwealth attorney, commenced in Wythville, Va., April 30, 1912. Some jurors were swayed by Floyd's plea that he drew his gun in self defense, but a verdict of guilty to first degree murder was finally rendered after two no agreements on May 18, 1912.

During the next two months, Claude Allen faced three separate trials, one for the death of the judge and two for the death of the commonwealth attorney. His plea, "I shot to protect my father," struggled for the compassion of the jurors, but their hearts and minds heeded also the prosecution's demand for retribution. Five people, in the service of the court, were dead; thirty-two children were fatherless.

In the first trial Claude was found guilty of murder in the second degree for the death of the judge. The jury of the trial for the death of the commonwealth attorney could not reach a verdict and was dismissed. A wearying re-trial finally reached its denouement late in July. Claude Allen rose to hear the jury foreman speak the words that condemned him to the fate of his father, death in the electric chair.

Time had an ameliorating effect benefitting the four remaining defendants. At trials held later in the year, they received prison terms ranging from eighteen to thirty-five years.

Many Virginia citizens believed that the death sentences for Floyd and Claude should be reduced to life imprisonment and petitioned the governor. But, after several stays of execution, father and son died in the electric chair, March 28, 1913. Each went bravely to his death.

"Life is sweet, and we had rather live, if possible, but since death must come, I am not afraid to die." —from the final statement of Claude Allen.

Petitions on behalf of the remaining Allens and Edwards brought them pardons, the last to Sidna Allen in 1926 from the state prison in Richmond, Virginia.

Before his imprisonment, Sidna was a prosperous landowner and merchant. All his wealth was seized to aid the victims of the shoot-out.

While a prisoner, Sidna made a collection of tables, ornate treasure boxes, and other items from salvaged wood. One table contained 7,500 separate pieces.

Shortly after his release, Sidna began displaying his collection at fairs and exhibitions throughout the region, and made an economic comeback.

"This will not be the last of me," Sidna Allen said on being sent to prison.

Crossing under Parkway
200.8 miles
no access

There is no access to Interstate 77 as it crosses under the Blue Ridge at this point.

View of Granite Quarry
202.8 miles
elev. 3,015

All mountains are not seen. Some lie buried. The slash of white, dimly visible in the lowlands, is the Mount Airy granite quarry. A veritable submerged mountain of granite, enough stone lies in deposits to produce 3,000 carloads per year for more than 500 years. Composed of evenly distributed white feldspar, blue-gray quartz, and black mica, the granite is a uniform grayish white appropriate for monuments, state buildings, and bridges.

Well-known examples are the Wright Brothers Memorial at Kitty Hawk, N.C., and the Arlington Memorial Bridge at Washington, D.C.

The entire expanse of lowlands below lies within the "Old Belt," the first section of the South developed for flue-cured tobacco.

View of the Piedmont
203.9 miles
elev. 2,900

The piedmont is a broad geographic area of rolling terrain extending southwesterly through Virginia and the Carolinas. It is bounded by the mountains on the west and the level tidewater region on the east.

Piper Gap
206.1 miles
elev. 2,759

Mountain gaps are named for a variety of reasons, but generally their names originate from an early settler who lived in the immediate vicinity. A road or trail usually led through the gap and acquired the same name. These "roads" that twisted up and down the mountains were at first very ordinary affairs. Some were barely improvements over a former elk or buffalo trail.

During the mid-1800s, local folks began to clamor for better roads. Of first importance was a better road between the county seats of Mt. Airy, N.C., and Independence, Va. To meet this need came Col. James H. Piper, a civil engineer. He located the new road according to scientific methods rather than the whims of a bull buffalo.

Hanks Branch
212.2 miles
Trout stream

New River drainage into the Gulf of Mexico.

The Hanks for whom the stream is named are believed to be kinfolk of Nancy Hanks Lincoln, the mother of "Honest Abe."

Low Gap
215.8 miles
elev. 2,416

Va. Rt. 89. Galax, Va.; 7 miles north; Mt. Airy, N.C., 22 miles east; Hanging Rock State Park, 48 miles east.

As its name suggests, Low Gap traverses the mountains at an elevation lower than any nearby crossing. It could just as appropriately be named for the galax plant, glory ground-cover of the Appalachians. The forested borders of the roadway near and below the gap are fringed with their patent-leather luster.

Galax grows in evergreen carpets of heart-shaped leaves beneath dense canopies of rhododendron and mountain laurel. In June-July the star-bright flowers sparkle on wandlike stems above their dark, leafy background. Spots of sunlight penetrating the darkness of the "rhododendron night" make the white blossoms glisten like a milky way, like a galaxy of stars. In forest openings, where the late summer sun can reach the leaves, they turn a deep maroon. Throughout the year the leaves are gathered in the woods by "pickers." Each packs his leaves in a burlap bag, totes them home, and ties them into bundles of 25.

Low Gap, N.C., a town below the Blue Ridge, is a

GALAX

purchasing center. Local merchants buy them by the thousands. Some are shipped directly to florists who use them in wreaths and other decorations. Other leaves are treated with dyes and sold as souvenirs.

**Galax, Va.,
Home of the Old
Fiddlers'
Convention**
*7 miles north on Va.
Rt. 89*

FIDDLE

Galax is a thriving city named for the mountain flower with the evergreen leaf. Galax is the congenial host for several summer events but one in particular has a sound all its own.

As the homefolks will tell you, the feet of old-time music lovers begin twitching come the first day of August. Come the second weekend in August, all roads lead to Galax for the Old Fiddlers' Convention. Sponsored by the Loyal Order of Moose, it began as a one night stand in Galax High School in 1935; but it caught on and grew because all of us homefolks wanted it to.

Contestants come from farm or factory, city or town, college campus or retirement condo. Some never had a lesson. They just started as tadpoles and took their daddy's fiddle off the wall and never stopped playing. Some are schooled in the concert manner of the great guitarist Segovia. All are lured to Galax by a common love for the ever-living music of yesterday.

Out in the parking lot of Felts Park the musicians get tuned up to come on stage. Close at hand you can hear the fiddle, the banjo, the mandolin, the guitar, and the dulcimer. And maybe you'll see some young flatfoot dancer, too shy to try the big time, clog away to the tunes just as if no one was watching.

But on stage is where it's at: "Fisher's Hornpipe," "John Henry," "Turkey in the Straw," "Bile Them Cabbage Down," "Old Joe Clark," and "Black Mountain Rag." Can't you just hear it?

**The Rooftop of
Virginia Crafts**

Grayson County, astride the state line, is the home of Mount Rogers (elev. 5,729), the highest mountain in Virginia.

Native craftsmen, under a program administered by the Federal Community Action Agency, provide handicrafts to the Rooftop of Virginia Crafts with outlets in Galax, Grayson Highlands State Park, and the Mount Rogers National Recreation area of the Jefferson National Forest.

**Chestnut Creek,
West Fork**
216.0 miles

Trout stream; New River drainage into Gulf of Mexico.

State Line
216.9 miles

In 1749 a party including Peter Jefferson and Joshua Fry surveyed the Virginia-North Carolina line across the Blue Ridge. Peter Jefferson was the father of a famous red-haired son named Thomas. Peter and Joshua Fry were well known mapmakers of their time.

**Cumberland Knob
Recreation Area
*217.9 miles***

Rest rooms; picnic grounds; water fountains; hiking trails.

Cumberland Knob is the Parkway's first recreation area and, along with the section of motor road extending 12.7 miles south from the state line, marks the Parkway's great beginning. The contract for road construction was awarded by the Bureau of Public Roads in 1935 and completed the following year. At its inception, the Parkway was a Depression-era project of the Roosevelt administration. Workers, other than supervisory personnel, were hired from the relief roles of local Allegheny County. Barring the inevitable exceptions, they were eager to be employed and freed from the onus of welfare. Whenever possible, local materials were used to aid the local economy.

Cumberland Knob recreation area developed from the youthful energies of the Civilian Conservation Corps, 1936-37. Young men from America's cities, towns, and farms worked out of a nearby camp to build the picnic grounds and lay the miles of trails over the Knob and along the shady course of Gully Creek.

Cumberland Knob (elev. 2,885) probably derives its name from William Augustus, duke of Cumberland (1721-1765), victor in the battle of Culloden, Scotland, 1746. The duke led an army of Scottish lowlanders and English against Scottish highlanders loyal to "Bonnie Prince Charlie," the Stewart claimant to the English crown. Duke William became a hero to the English and an object of hatred to the highland Scots. In England a showy garden flower, the Sweet William, was named in his honor. The highlanders dubbed a species of ragwort as "stinking Willie," in acerbic reply.

In America, the years immediately following Cumberland's victory were a time of westward expansion and exploration by the English. As objects of English pride, towns, counties, forts, rivers, and mountains were named for the duke. In colonial times, Cumberland County, Virginia, embraced a huge area including the land adjacent to Cumberland Knob.

FLOWERING DOGWOOD

BLACK OR PITCH PINE

Forest Trees and Shrubs
Predominantly oak mixed with other broad-leaf trees and
pines; rosebay rhododendron, mountain laurel, leuco-
thoe understory; galax ground cover.

scarlet oak	Virginia pine	mountain
red oak	serviceberry	laurel
chestnut oak	pignut hickory	deerberry
white oak	persimmon	minniebush
black oak	yellow poplar	dwarf sumac
red maple	or tulip tree	red-twig
sweet or black	black gum	leucothoe
birch	rosebay	alternate-leaved
white pine	rhododendron	dogwood
pitch or black	flowering	flame azalea
pine	dogwood	withe-rod
table mountain	sassafras	viburnum
pine	pink azalea	smooth sumac
	winterberry	

Ground Flowers

galax	purple bluet	venus looking
rattlesnake	bowman's root	glass
hawkweed	silverrod	whorled
dyer's-weed	wave aster	loosestrife
goldenrod		catfoot

WOOD PEEWEE

Birds and Other Wildlife

turkey vulture	brown	robin
ruffed grouse	thrasher	wood thrush
bobwhite	catbird	chipping
mourning dove	Carolina wren	sparrow
blue jay	tufted titmouse	field sparrow
crested	ovenbird	goldfinch
flycatcher	yellow-breasted	indigo bunting
wood pewee	chat	towhee
phoebe	prairie	gray squirrel
downy	warbler	chipmunk
woodpecker	parula warbler	cottontail
red-headed	black-and-white	fencepost
woodpecker	warbler	lizard
flicker	ruby-throated	
	hummingbird	

FLICKER

CAROLINA WREN

Fox Hunter's
Paradise
218.6 miles
elev. 2,805

Picnic table; sweet fern, and chinquapin in parking
area; trail.

This celestial name applies to a fox hunter's rendezvous
of cherished regard that the hunters themselves knew as
High Piney Spur. A short trail from the parking area ends
by a log bench and a seven-leagues look of the countryside. The crest of High Piney drops away and then tips up

to form a forested knoll before descending like a long arm into the lowlands. On this knoll the fox hunters used to gather and listen to the music of their hounds, hot on the trail.

Some hunters made it a family affair and the occasion for a picnic. After darkness drew nigh, " 'long about the edge of the evening," they set the dogs loose and enjoyed the chase with their wives and young'uns and perhaps a neighbor or two.

For the most part, however, fox hunting has always been a man's-night-out sport: gathering with his chums on places like High Piney to test the skill of his dogs.

Fox hunting, mountain style, is an unusual "spectator sport." The ears, not the eyes, are most important for following the hunt. To enjoy a hunt a man must know the country and have a good dog.

Set loose, the hounds run off, noses to the ground after the scent. They seldom go far before striking a trail. Then the music begins in full voice. "Hear that music?" asked a hunter of a friend who had come to the hunt out of curiosity. "I don't hear no music," came the reply, "all I hear is those dogs a-barkin.' "

Although hunters cherish a dog with a resounding voice, they want no part of a "babbler." Such hounds bay up a storm for no particular reason and have a tendency to roam far off the trail. They get too excited for their own good, and confuse the issue. Sometimes a dog that knows the country and the habits of the fox too well may become a "cutter." This canny type figures out the course the fox will travel and takes short cuts, much to the displeasure of its master. And, of course, no hunter wants his dog to be a "quitter," but to stay after the fox all night if need be.

The idea of the hunt is to listen to the hounds and have your entry "top dog" and in the lead. No one cares about catching the fox.

The fox usually sees to that, and allows the dogs a merry chase but finally dens up or gives them the slip. Often the fox seems to enjoy a good run and leads the dogs for mile-long scampers. Tiring of the exercise, the fox resorts to stratagems. Favored ruses are running along highways and over newly plowed land, traveling atop rail fences, and following streams.

Occasionally the hounds will corner the fox. After brief violence the quarry is a limp piece of fur and the hunt is over.

Of the two species of foxes in the mountains, the red is preferred. The gray fox doesn't care for the chase and will den up after a short run.

Big Pine Creek
222.3-225.1 miles

Big Pine meanders along the Parkway for a few miles then turns northwest and enters Little River, a tributary of the New. It is a good trout stream, with large white and pitch pines growing along the banks.

Hare Mill Pond
225.2 miles
elev. 2,590

COTTONTAIL

The Hare Mill, dating back to Civil War times, led a busy life prior to the construction of the Parkway. It stood on the present site of the motor road. Through the years, the various owners operated a combination of gristmills, saws, an end-grooved flooring plane, and a jointer.

As a profitable sideline they bought thousands of rabbits, known locally as "hares," from local trappers and hunters, and sold them to nearby market centers such as Mount Airy, N.C.

Roaring Gap
229.7 miles
elev. 2,700

U.S. 21 Sparta 7 miles north, Elkin 25 miles south. Home of the roaring winter wind.

Little Glade Pond
230.1 miles
elev. 2,709

BULL FROG

Loop trail; roadside easel: the living pond; picnic tables.
Mitten-shaped Little Glade Pond offers the fisherman a chance to try his luck. Rainbow trout and bluegill rise to the bait—if the lure strikes their fancy.

The Parkway built the pond near the site of an old "tub," or turbine-type mill, operated about 1895-1915. The water power came by way of a long mill race from Little Glade Creek. The steady volume from the stream made it unnecessary to build a mill pond. The mill stones were quarried from the excellent granite of Stone Mountain.

Stone Mountain View
232.5 miles
elev. 3,115

Virginia pine, pitch pine, table mountain pine, red cedar.
Stone Mountain lies to the left along the foothills, inconspicuous in size, but at once distinctive for its furrowed slopes of bare, almost white, granite rock. The dome-shaped mountain is the remnant of a batholith, a great mass of molten granite that hardened considerably below the earth's surface. In time it was exposed by erosion.

Stone Mountain has always been a much visited "curiosity." A pair of water-worn grooves, roughly parallel, conjure speculation about giant wagon tracks, grooved into the rock by a legendary wagoner. Small water-worn pockets along the way resemble the tracks of huge oxen. Another feature is the "rat-eat" rock, gnawed by the elements so as to resemble the front of an overturned auto.

Once a party of visitors came to explore the summit. One of the men lost his footing along the edge and pitched headlong down the slick sides. Just before plunging to his death down a vertical drop of 200 feet he caught a tree, escaping with bruises and future nightmares.

View of Bullhead Mountain
233.7 miles
elev. 3,200

A forested, loaf-shaped mountain, (elev. 3,850), with a "bull's head" apparent along its crest, particularly on the side opposite the Parkway. According to a local-color tale a group of men came upon a bull on the mountain belonging to a neighbor they did not like. Out of "pure mean-

ness'' they pinned the bull's head between the forks of a tree and left it there to die. *(Clay Caudill, 1956)*

Deep Gap
234.1 miles
elev. 3,193

This crossing of an old wagon road between the plateau community of Whitehead and Elkin in the foothills is known by the rangers as Deep Gap of the Bullhead, to distinguish it from the Deep Gap forty-two miles southwest.

Mahogany Rock
235.1 miles
elev. 3,436

red oak	*white pine*
chestnut oak	*black locust*
pignut	*red maple*
white ash	*sweet birch*

Mahogany Rock stands across the motor road from the overlook like an ingrown toenail in the stump of a sweet birch, or mahogany tree. Fin-shaped rock outcrops are common throughout the plateau region, particularly at Rocky Knob and Doughton Park recreation areas. An old mahogany tree once grew above this particular rock-fin and became a wind-blown landmark known as Mahogany Rock.

BLACK OR SWEET BIRCH

From the overlook spreads a sweeping survey of the Blue Ridge plateau. The rolling terrain of the Virginia portion on the right contrasts with the abruptly mountainous Carolina scene.

Immediately below is the Pine Swamp section, the home of Carolina Joines who became Mrs. Martin Brinegar at age 15. In the background stretches the crest line of the Peach Bottom Mountains, whose lower slopes were formerly covered with peach trees. As the range dips near the Virginia line, it points out the classically named town of Sparta, N.C.

In the far distance, beyond the hulking forms of several mountains, is the long outline of the Iron range, forming the western border of the Blue Ridge plateau along the Great Valley.

Devil's Garden
235.7 miles
elev. 3,428

A "gunsight" view aims between two slopes into the Piedmont lowlands. The rocky, stunted picture reveals a "devil's garden." Mountaineers often gave the devil's name to rough, rocky features. In Virginia a sharp-edged spur, largely barren of trees along its "spine," is the Devil's Backbone. The Devil's Courthouse is a high, rocky summit on Pisgah Ledge, south of Asheville.

Devil's Garden is a well-deserved term for a more sinister reason than mere rockiness. Rattlesnakes and copperheads are abundant. Both of these venomous reptiles are pit vipers, so called because of a pair of nostril-like pits just below their eyes. They contain organs supersensitive to heat, by means of which the snakes locate warm-blooded prey.

Both species are readily distinguished from the various harmless mountain snakes by their heavy bodies and flat, diamond-shaped heads. The unblinking eyes, with the slitlike pupils of a cat, give them a terrifying appearance, particularly when they are ''quile-ed up'' and poised to strike.

The smaller and appropriately named copperhead is often regarded with more fear than the rattler because of its fighting nature and lack of the warning rattle. It is usually found below the mountains, but a few climb to 4,000 feet.

The native rattler is the common timber rattler of the East. They were formerly found in great numbers throughout the mountains and are by no means rare today. Generally they are most abundant in deserted areas like the Devil's Garden. Here the ''buzz-tails'' lurk beneath a rock ledge or blueberry bush, waiting to ambush their favorite prey of mice and rats.

The rattler's habit of shaking the rattle on the end of its tail is not given as a warning, but is merely a nervous reaction. Other species, including the blacksnake, also vibrate their tails when excited. Considering the sound on its own merits, it is innocent enough, something like a baby's rattle. But to have one ''sing'' too close by is enough to dry the marrow of your bones.

TIMBER RATTLESNAKE

According to a former park ranger, rattlers can be rendered unconscious by switching them. He claims to have mastered the snakes on numerous occasions in this manner, but is fond of relating one particular occasion. Seeing a rattler nearby, poised to strike, he cut a switch from a birch tree and smote the reptile a stinging blow. The confused snake tried to crawl away from its unknown torment, right between the ranger's legs. ''What did you do then?'' comes the inevitable question. Says the ranger, ''I clumb the switch!''

Snake stories are legion throughout the mountains. Luckily nearly all are of the humorous scare type. Long ago, a young fellow came hurrying home along a mountain trail. It was approaching dusk, the time when rattlers are most about, and, for certain, they were very much on his mind.

Suddenly he came upon a big one. The snake struck him just as he broke into a run for his life. Home was several miles away but he ran every inch of it. Home at last, he made the nerve-shattering discovery that the rattler still clung to his pants. But the snake was dead-limp. The fangs had hooked into his much patched trouser seat. Unable to release itself, the snake had been beaten to death against trees, bushes, and rocks that the young fellow brushed against in his dash for home.

Many mountaineers have a dread of rattlers. But not ''Rattlesnake'' Sam Crishawm. Sam flourished about a half century ago near the Parkway in the vicinity of Gillespie Gap, mile 331. Sam led a normal enough life until his family had grown, and then he assumed a more solitary existence. For company he kept a rattler or two, often allowing the reptile the freedom of the house. His attachment for the snakes was not of the morbid variety; he merely understood them and saw no reason for being fearful. When in need of cash, Sam sold rattlers to medicine men at county fairs by the pound.

Evidently he learned a trick or two from the medicine men, for Sam prescribed a potent remedy for TB. The ''cure'' consisted of good moonshine containing portions of rattlesnake, ''killed when it was in a happy frame of mind.''

The native rattler occurs in two color phases, the yellow and the black. Both phases have a velvety black tail, giving them the nickname of ''velvet-tip.'' An average rattler will measure about three feet, but some exceed fifty inches. A true mountaineer, the timber rattler may be found at elevations well over 5,000 feet.

View from Air Bellows Gap
236.9 miles
elev. 3,744

The view, like that from Mahogany Rock, embraces parallel tiers of mountain ranges etched from the Blue Ridge plateau by the New River. The north and the south forks of the river lie behind the long ranges in the background.

Air Bellows Gap
237.1 miles
elev. 3,929

A very windy place, particularly in winter when the snowdrifts pile. The road through the gap, like countless others of its kind, was built and maintained by the local residents. Martin Brinegar used it in his yearly travels to pay his taxes in Wilkesboro. Travel by wagon was possible only in ''good'' weather, so folks generally walked or rode horseback. *(Ross Reeves, 1956)*

Today practically all local roads are maintained by the state.

Brinegar Cabin
238.5 miles
elev. 3,508

Handicraft exhibit and local lore demonstrations.

Martin Brinegar (1856-1925) and his child bride, the former Caroline Joines (1863-1943) settled on their newly purchased farm about 1880. For several years, man and wife worked at raising crops, clearing land, and building up their livestock and poultry.

In 1885 Martin began a five-year span of building the present homestead: cabin, barn, shed, and spring house. The Brinegars were immensely proud of their spring, always ''two degrees cooler than the mornin.'''

Except for help in placing the house logs, Martin did all the work himself. In spring he planted the crops, and during the summer worked on the buildings. Caroline and her young family tended the farm. The Brinegars raised crops typical of the surrounding countryside: corn, buckwheat, rye, oats, wheat, potatoes, turnips, and sorghum.

The stock ''ran the mountains'' in common with the neighbors', but marked by a swallowtail fork in each ear.

Brinegar Cabin

During fall, at harvest time, the Brinegars cut their cereal crops with a hand scythe or "reap hook," and threshed the grain by flailing it with a hickory pole. The flailing end of the hickory was shredded so that the fibers acted like numerous whips to beat the grain out of its hull.

RAZORBACK HOG

Fall was also the time Caroline preferred for weaving with her big "four-poster" loom, built by Daddy Ezekiel Joines as a wedding present. With linen thread and woolen yarn she wove the durable "linsey-woolsey" cloth that made the "lastingest garments there war." During times when thread was "hard to come by," Caroline raised her own flax.

Caroline did not read or write, but she could interpret the old timey "tromped as writ" patterns for her loom. These resembled sheet music. Symbols like musical notes indicated which of the foot treadles to tromp to weave the pattern.

The Brinegars, like most mountain people of their day, had very little cash. But since they were largely self-sufficient, their need for dollars probably came to less than a few hundred a year. They satisfied this need by a "money crop." Caroline and the children collected herbs. The roots of bloodroot, May apple, black snakeroot and alumroot, and the bark of wild cherry, shonny haw (withe-rod viburnum), and white pine were gathered and sold to drug merchants in nearby Jefferson and Boone.

Martin earned his hard cash as a cobbler, making shoes for a dollar a pair, more or less, depending upon the size of the feet.

The most important activity of the Brinegar famly was its church. Martin served as clerk for the Pleasant Grove Baptist Church. He regularly attended the monthly services. They lasted for two days and made up for the lapse of Sunday services in between. The church forbade the playing of musical instruments at the services and Martin, therefore, forbade them in his house.

He also frowned on such frivolities as dancing, and "wouldn't allow a still on the place." The Brinegars were probably among the few folks on speaking terms with Steve Taylor, the local revenue officer.

Martin died in 1925 and Caroline lived on in her Blue Ridge cabin for over a decade until the land was purchased for the Parkway.

After Martin's death, Caroline befriended a black woman, who came to live with her for a while. For Caroline's excited appreciation, her friend would climb a tall tree and ride it "whoopingly" to the ground as neighbors chopped it down.

Her friends like to tell of Caroline's batting average against copperheads and rattlers. "Killed more than you could haul off in a wagon." Not "ary bit afraid," she killed them with anything at hand, be it a rock or a rail.

After the government acquired the property, Caroline moved to nearby Pine Swamp Valley where she lived her last years with daughter Rene. She spent many happy hours storytelling to her grandchildren. She spoke in a low confidential voice that not even the parents could hear. But they could tell by the laughter when it was about "funny people," or by the rapt silence when Granny was recalling tales of long ago full of wild animals and danger.

When things were quiet, she often sat in a rocker just behind the doorway half ajar. There she would rock and rock, idly playing with the house key hanging from a string around her neck and musing with the thoughts of age and silence.

Low Notch
239.9 miles
elev. 3,482

The mountains drop sharply to form a V-shaped notch through which an old trail formerly passed. When a traveler reached the notch he knew he was crossing the Blue Ridge crest line.

Throughout the Southern Highlands the term "gap" is used for a mountain pass. The term notch is typical of New England. Perhaps someone from the Green Mountains or the Berkshires once settled nearby and named the place. Or perhaps the scenery is so like that of New England's mountains that the name just came naturally.

Doughton Park
238.6-244.8 miles
6,000 acres

Naturalist program: campfire talks, nature walks.

239.3 miles

Camping and trailer areas.

241.1 miles

Coffee and souvenir shop; lodge; auto service; picnic grounds; rest rooms; water fountains; hiking; Caudill cabin exhibit; trails.

Doughton Park is a triangular area enclosed within converging ridges that descend from the Blue Ridge crest line. The triangle is bisected by Bluff Mountain and the ridge that trails down from it into the foothills. As you face eastward, the area on the left of the Bluff is drained by Basin Creek, the area on the right by Cove Creek. The entire forested lowlands within this ridge-formed barricade are known as Basin Cove.

Prior to 1951 the Park was known as The Bluffs, from its central high point. It became Doughton Park in honor of Robert Lee "Muley Bob" Doughton, longtime congressman (1911-53) from North Carolina's 9th district, and staunch friend of the Parkway.

The broad summit of Bluff Mountain and the surrounding uplands along the motor road are covered with meadows of redtop and clover. The tinkling song of the horned lark carries across the rail-fence boundaries. Sometimes an exuberant bird flies above the fat mahogany-red cattle and sings in one fluttering spot like its European relative, the skylark. Carolina juncos hop about the lodge and coffee shop, tame as pigeons but much more musical.

Deer are frequently seen near the motor road in the vicinity of Alligator Back overlook, just south of the Ice Rocks. The Ice Rocks, mile 242, form a cliff on the side of Bluff Mountain. Each winter the "seeps" on the rock face freeze into a hanging waterfall of ice.

WILDCAT OR BOBCAT

One of the most visited places in the area is Wildcat Rocks, where the "bobtails" used to den. A short trail from the parking area passes by a bronze plaque honoring Congressman Doughton and stretches uphill to a now famous view of Basin Cove. Fifteen hundred feet below is the wind-polished Caudill cabin, a dramatic example of isolation, "beyond the tellin' of it."

The question is often asked, "How did anyone manage to live there?" To hear Lonnie Caudill describe the manner of livelihood gives the impression of a dead-end frontier that stayed the hands of time. Lonnie is a son of Martin Caudill, the man who built the cabin about 1895.

"Poppa kept 10 to 15 acres cleared and in crops. We had lots of fruit trees and in the fall of the year we'd gather up chestnuts and walnuts. We raised sheep and cattle, and geese both for eatin' and their feathers. Plucked 'm three to four times a summer.

"Basin Cove was a place people free-ranged their hogs. A man took his brood sow and penned her in some chestnut orchard. After a spell he'd go back to put his brand on the shoats and knock the pen down. The old sow had got used to the place and wouldn't wander off. In the fall of the year everyone would go and get his pigs.

"We did our huntin' mostly in winter. Mostly too busy farmin' in summer. There was lots of trout. Of a night when the weather was hot, we'd gig for eels.

"We made most everything we needed. Poppa and Momma made baskets from oak splits, and made all our shoes. Momma wove lots of cloth on the loom at Grandpa Harrison's, a ways down on Basin Creek."

GIGGED EEL

Martin and his growing family lived in the cabin off and on for perhaps a score of years and then moved to another place nearer to Grandpa Harrison's. Shortly thereafter, in 1916, a disaster occurred throughout much of the southeast that none of the families in Basin Cove would ever forget.

"It started raining about noon on a Friday of July 1916. It got worse through the night and next day. Landslides began around noon Saturday. Whole half acres just started sliding with timber 'til they hit the hollow. The water would dam up for a spell and then bust through. It made a roaring noise just like thunder. The next day was quiet with a light rain a-blowin' from the east." But three people, including Lonnie's brother Cornelius, were dead.

The unoccupied Caudill cabin escaped damage, as it lay upstream. But many other homes were destroyed, including Grandpa Harrison's.

Several families decided to leave the cove after the disaster, but the resolute Harrison chose to remain. He moved his address to the nearby home of his kinsman, Ritter Caudill. Harrison's obituary reveals him to be a remarkable man in one respect.

"Harrison Caudill was born February 3, 1839, and departed this life September 15, 1924. His stay on earth was 85 years, 7 months, 12 days. He was married to Mary C. Tilley in 1857. Unto this union was born 6 children. The Lord saw fit to call his companion away to the better home leaving him with six children. He afterward married Sarah Tilley and unto them were born 16 children, 22 children in all. His second wife preceded him in death. Two or three years after the departure of his second wife, he married Alpha Wagoner. He labored hard through life and had much trouble and trials, but from the fruit he bore we feel assured that he is sweetly resting on the other shore with many of his loved ones gone before." *(30th Annual Session of Little River Baptist Association, October, 1924)*

Son Martin carried on the family tradition and sired a family of 16. Only a few, however, were born in the one-room cabin below Wildcat Rocks. Undoubtedly it would have been much too confining.

Another trail heads away from the parking area at Wildcat Rocks, looping to and from Fodderstack Mountain. It represents a hike of over a mile, some of it rather steep, but nonetheless a rewarding outdoors venture.

A short distance from the starting point is a shelf like rock outcrop studded with small rust-colored garnet crystals. A green matting of "resurrection moss" covers portions of the rocks. During dry spells the small plants seem to die. But with the first good rain they "resurrect" into fresh green.

The far end of the trail breaks into a clearing caused by a forest fire in 1935, now covered with the typical plant association that reclaims such land. Most of the shrubs are members of the heath family, and form a natural "heath garden" of rhododendron, blueberry, huckleberry, minniebush, mountain laurel, and leucothoe. Within the garden rise a few Table Mountain pines, "fire-burn" pioneers.

An apparent oddity is a small clump of large-toothed aspen directly on the trail. They form entire forests in many northern regions, but are extremely rare in the Southern Highlands.

Two interesting native trees, the Carolina hemlock and Frazer magnolia, occur along the trail, probably survivors of the fire that cleared the way for the fire-burn pioneers.

Forest Trees and Shrubs

Mixed hardwoods with white pine very abundant in campgrounds; rosebay and catawba rhododendron, mountain laurel, leucothoe, highbush blueberry, and cinnamon-bush understory.

ROSEBAY RHODODENDRON

CATAWBA RHODODENDRON

MOUNTAIN LAUREL

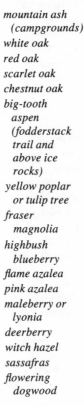

white pine
pitch or black
  pine
table
  mountain
  pine
Virginia pine
  (campgrounds)
eastern
  hemlock
  (campgrounds)
Carolina
  hemlock
  (fodderstack
  trail)
rosebay
  rhododendron
catawba
  rhododendron
mountain
  laurel
leucothoe
cinnamonbush
minniebush
alternate-leaved
  dogwood

mountain ash
  (campgrounds)
white oak
red oak
scarlet oak
chestnut oak
big-tooth
  aspen
  (fodderstack
  trail and
  above ice
  rocks)
yellow poplar
  or tulip tree
fraser
  magnolia
highbush
  blueberry
flame azalea
pink azalea
maleberry or
  lyonia
deerberry
witch hazel
sassafras
flowering
  dogwood

cucumber tree
yellow birch
sweet or black
  birch
red maple
striped maple
  (campgrounds)
black or sour
  gum
persimmon
white ash
black cherry
pignut
black locust
serviceberry
mountain
  winterberry
wild
  hydrangea
American
  elder
staghorn
  sumac
  (trailer
  camp)
dwarf sumac
  (campgrounds)

List continues

Ground Flowers

Spring

violet
buttercup
great
  chickweed
painted
  trillium
wild geranium
common
  cinquefoil

blue-eyed
  grass
may apple
solomon's
  seal
speckled
  wood-lily
solomon's
  plume
sundrop
bluet

blackberry
field
  hawkweed
dewberry
spiderwort
fire-pink
bowman's
  root
small's
  ragwort

TOWHEE

Summer

fly-poison
galax
wood
  coreopsis
star coreopsis
heal-all
black-eyed
  susan
daisy fleabane

spotted star
  thistle
star campion
yarrow
purple bluet
smooth
  gerardia
touch-me-not
butterfly weed

blazing star
yellow indigo
alumroot
virgins bower,
  or clematis
common
  milkweed
New Jersey
  tea

CAROLINA JUNCO

Fall

dyer's-weed
  goldenrod
field
  goldenrod
curtis
  goldenrod

white wood
  aster
tall goldenrod
white
  snakeroot

catfoot
wave aster
silverrod
crownbeard

RUFFED GROUSE

Common Ferns

hay-scented
cinnamon
polypody

New York
Christmas
marginal
  shield

interrupted
lady
rattlesnake

Birds and Other Wildlife

turkey vulture
bobwhite
ruffed grouse
crow
wood thrush
robin
kingbird
wood pewee
ruby-throated
  hummingbird
black-throated
  blue warbler
blackburnian
  warbler
Canadian
  warbler

black-throated
  green
  warbler
ovenbird
goldfinch
towhee
indigo bunting
field sparrow
chipping
  sparrow
Carolina
  junco
scarlet
  tanager
mourning
  dove

downy
  woodpecker
flicker
cedar
  waxwing
chimney swift
blue-headed
  vireo
brown
  thrasher
horned lark
black-capped
  chickadee
gray squirrel
Virginia
  white-tailed
  deer

CARPET MOSS

PIGEON WHEAT

FRINGE—LEAF MOSS

BROOM MOSS

FERN MOSS

The Alligator Back is an elongated outcrop of gneiss extending along the motor road. Its fancied resemblance to the ''ole gator'' shows the influence of ''picture-story'' books.

The parking area has a large color-coded map of the Doughton Park Trail System. One of the trails takes you for an hour's hike to Bluff Mountain and back. You begin through mast-straight trunks of black locust encumbered with bittersweet vines. You enter a forest where trees pry upward through a dark green maze of rosebay rhododendron. The way is cool, dark, and always with the presence of a breeze. The mountain boomer, or red squirrel, is a scampering scold. Juncos, vague as the shade they dwell in, create occasional sounds and movement.

Mosses trim the wayside, spreading in cushions and tussocks among the leaf litter, draping over rotting logs and stumps, covering a ledge with a forest of miniature evergreens, clinging like damp fur to the vertical face of wet rocks.

If you have an extra hour to spare, stop at places where mosses are abundant and see if you can identify them using the following descriptions and border illustrations:

White moss, *Leucobryum,* resembles greenish-white ''pin-cushions'' among the leaf-litter at the base of trees. They are whiter in dry weather, greener with rain.

Pigeon wheat, *Polytrichium,* stands like a tiny forest of upright spruce twigs. Slender stems project from the top of each plant bearing a spore-case shaped like a grain of wheat. The spores sift out in dry weather for a chance landing and a chance to develop into moss.

Various *Hypnum* or carpet mosses spread an interweaving mat over soil or decaying wood. Their green has a golden cast, even in shade. Fern moss, *Thuidium,* intermingles with carpet moss on mouldering logs and stumps. It rises over the recumbent carpet moss, feathery and fernlike.

Broom moss, *Dicranum,* grows in luxuriant, glossy crowds over a forest floor rich in humus. The leaves along the stem tend to point in one general direction. The long-stalked spore cases also tend to point one way and resemble a flock of long-necked birds looking toward a source of sudden interest.

The yellowish fringe-leaf moss, *Hedwigia,* adheres to moist rocks. The tiny hairlike leaf tips are whitish, giving a hoary cast. The olive-green to blackish *Grimmia* is another rock dweller. On exposed mountaintop rocks its fragile patches are repeatedly detached by the wind. But nothing has more perseverance than moss.

The top of Bluff Mountain is just ahead, an open rocky outcrop that testifies to the violence of the wind. Catawba rhododendron replaces the rosebay. Soil is scoured from the rocks and pushed into pockets where a few stubborn and tattered shrubs persist. But the soil is rich and water is plentiful explaining the presence of the fringe tree. It grows more commonly and much less rigorously in damp woods south to Florida. It also has the resources to sustain itself on exposed mountain bluffs. In May the shrub is festooned with strands of white blossoms.

The path leads to a broad mountaintop meadow through an open gate in the rail fence that permits passage to hikers but not to cattle. You will readily see why. The meadow reaches a mile or so toward Bluffs Lodge. You may see Herefords grazing and paying you no mind. Just ahead is a trail shelter on a level stretch with a view and a chance to take ten.

Bluff Mountain
Overlook
243.4 miles
elev. 3,334

Bluff Mountain (elev. 3,785), with its sheer rock wall and patches of clinging forest, shows on the left. Bluff Ridge gradually descends from the mountain, merging finally into Basin Cove. Cedar "Clifts," long and rocky, lies just across the way.

The summit of Bluff Mountain is remarkably broad and level, covered by a meadow over a mile to Bluff Lodge. A road from Doughton Park picnic grounds reaches these brisk and sparkling heights and a sweeping survey of the countryside.

On the right lies Flat Rock Ridge, the second of two flat-topped heights extending from the Parkway. Here the Blevins, Caudills, Bells, and the other hardy folks of Basin Cove came to "course for bees." The honey hunter placed a mixture of manure and water in one of the pot-like holes scoured by the elements on Flat Rock. This foul-smelling "stink bait" attracted the bees as though it were a rosebush. Corncobs were stuck in the bait to prevent the bees from falling in and drowning.

HONEYBEE ON A CORNCOB

After time to enable the bees to learn the location of the bait, the courser would climb up to the Flat Rock and begin his coursin'. Along came a bee, paying a visit to the bait. Then, mission accomplished, it took off in a beeline for its hive. The courser followed its flight, making note of where the bee disappeared. If it seemed headed for a place reasonably near, he chose a point farther along the bee's route and watched for others to come buzzing by. If successful, he would be led to the hive.

Most coursing was done late in the summer when the bees had built up a good supply of honey. Earlier in the year folks were on the lookout to capture a swarm and take the bees home. An early swarm made lots of honey; a late swarm barely made the effort to capture them worthwhile.

A swarm in May is worth a load of hay.
A swarm in June is worth a silver spoon.
A swarm in July ain't worth a fly.

View of
Basin Cove
244.7 miles
elev. 3,312

Cove Creek below and Basin Creek on the yonder side of Bluff Ridge to the immediate left drain the sprawling foothills of Basin Cove.

On the far left the patchily bald head of Stone Mountain

WHITE-TAILED DEER

domes up below a long spur extending from the Blue Ridge. From this far point to a distance of several miles on the right, the forested foothills surrounding Doughton Park comprise the state of North Carolina's Thurmond-Chatham Game Lands.

Its successful game management program enables Parkway visitors to enjoy the sight of a graceful white-tailed deer bounding along the roadside meadows. The deer are frequently seen near the overlook after five o'clock in the evening.

Meadow Fork Valley
246.5-248.1 miles

Meadow Fork Creek, trout stream, New River tributary, Gulf of Mexico drainage.

The stream flows over a valley unusually level and broad for an area so close to the mountain crest line.

The forested side of the motor road contains a garden understory of flowering shrubs. May and June are colorful with dogwood, pink and flame azalea, purple rhododendron, and the flat white clusters of withe-rod viburnum, or shonny haw.

N.C. Rt. 18
248.1 miles
elev. 2,851

North Wilkesboro 25 miles southeast; Sparta 15 miles north.

Alder Gap
251.5 miles
elev. 3,047

The alder *(Alnus serrulata)* of the mountains forms a dense shrub-border along streams. It has a habit of taking over moist meadows, much to the displeasure of the farmer who wants the land for pasture. Alders are the first shrubs to bloom in spring, the greenish flowers appearing in March, almost a month before the leaves. A tea tonic is brewed from the leaves and bark. According to local herb gatherer Cora Camp, it "richens the blood."

Jess Sheets Cabin
252.5 miles

Andrew Sheets came to America from Germany, during or shortly after the Revolutionary War. He landed in Virginia and later came to North Carolina. According to family tradition, several of Andrew's sons moved into the mountains sometime thereafter. Son Jess reputedly built this one-room cabin about 1815.

Several generations of Sheetses lived in it up to the time the state bought the property for the Parkway. The young ones went to Peak Creek school house, about a mile away. On the average they "just lacked three or four days of gettin' about three months schoolin'."

Sheets Gap Overlook
252.8 miles
elev. 3,342

The forest fringe around the overlook contains several Frazer magnolias, one of the loveliest blossoms of May. The pink bud-sheath unpeels, revealing the languid loveliness of cream-colored flowers, five to seven inches across. In August the velvet-red fruit catches the eyes of visitors, poking out from the umbrella-like leaves.

Beyond the forested foothills that stretch from the Blue

Ridge lie the levels of the Yadkin Valley, framed on the far horizon by the Brushy Mountains. The panorama is an excellent storyteller of Blue Ridge geology. The long rows of spurs or foothills end abruptly in a generally straight line, and mark the former location of the Blue Ridge crest.

In the way-long-ago, the earth's surface cracked along this line. The land on this side uplifted; the land on the other side, including the Brushy Mountains, held the old height. The high face of the resultant cliff, several hundred miles long, formed the ancient Blue Ridge.

During the ages since, stream action has broadened the Yadkin Valley and carved the spurlike foothills below. This is still in progress. The Blue Ridge crest, or watershed divide between the Atlantic and the Gulf of Mexico, is ever so gradually being shifted westward by these hard-cutting, eastward-flowing cascades.

You might wonder what will become of the slower Gulf-bound streams flowing over the Plateau. Ultimately they will be "pirated" into the drainage system of the Atlantic.

FRASER MAGNOLIA

Northwest Trading Post
258.6 miles

The Northwest Trading Post has local color on its shelves. Hewed from the imagination and perseverance of Ashe County citizens, the trading post deals in the home products of Ashe and ten neighboring counties of northwest North Carolina.

> Wooden ware with the whittler's mark,
> Woven rugs dyed from maple bark,
> Pickled dilly beans, country ham,
> Dewberry jelly, strawberry jam,
> White oak baskets, split-bottom chairs,
> Convey the aroma of country fairs.
> Craftsman styled, made by hand,
> They sing the song of the mountain land.

SPLIT-BOTTOM CHAIR

Jumpin' Off Rocks
260.3 miles
elev 3,165
Picnic table, trail

red oak	*white pine*
scarlet oak	*dogwood*
white oak	*rosebay*
red maple	*rhododendron*
yellow poplar	*mountain laurel*
black locust	*clematis vine.*
pignut	

The trail (.5 mile) is a walk to the Jumpin'-Off Rocks and a jumpin'-off view. The path is fringed on its high side by trailing arbutus, and passes through lustrous, dark green pools of galax.

Cinnamon-colored bark identifies the cinnamonbush or pepperbush. The seed pod can be ground into a powder and used as a condiment. The cinnamonbush, like the locally common sourwood tree, blooms in late summer. Each has white clusters of small, urn-shaped flowers.

SOURWOOD

The sourwood is a "leaner" tree. Not tall enough to compete with the dominant forest trees, it leans into available areas of sunlight. When it locates its place in the sun, it bends and grows upward. Do you see any such sourwood trees? For years mountain farmers have used sourwood trunks to make sled runners.

Mountain farmers use sleds for hauling, summer and winter. Sleds can be hauled over the steep land easier than a wagon and they seldom tip over. The trunk of a sourwood with a bend in it makes a good sled runner.

Horse Gap
261.2 miles
elev. 3,108

N.C. Rt. 16; North Wilkesboro, 25 miles southeast; Jefferson, 12 miles northwest.

Sometimes things like this just happen. Apparently none of the nearby natives ever heard of Horse Gap until the Parkway placed a sign. The name appeared on a U.S. Geological Survey map dated 1891 marking a mountain crossing a short distance south. During the 1930s when N.C. 16 was relocated along its present route, the state applied Horse Gap to its present site.

Daniel Gap
262.3 miles
elev. 3,167

A wagon road from Jefferson to Wilkesboro crossed the Blue Ridge at Daniel Long's. Long and his partner, Lyon, operated a store about 1890-1910. Many of their customers exchanged farm produce and herbs collected from the mountains for drygoods, kerosene, and maybe something fancy like candy jawbreakers.

Every now and then the two men loaded up burlap bags of herbs and hauled them to Wilkesboro for sale to the drug companies. The road was so rough the team had to be rested every few miles.

View from the Lump
264.4 miles
elev. 3,465

"This here's my favorite lookout," said Uncle Newt. "Afore the Parkway ever was thought of I'd come here and set out, just a-lookin' at the view. I just come to set awhile and collect my thoughts. It's so green and purty lookin'.

"Sometimes, of a night, fox hunters had'm a sociable here. They'd set thur hounds loose and then just lazy around a fire list'nen to them hounds a-bayin'.

"The Lump's kindly a natural name. Hit's just a big, round hill stickin' up thar and folks began callin' it The Lump right on. Close agin' it on the fur side's a smaller one knowed as the Little Lump.

"This here's what I call a 'pitchin' view, a-swoopin' into all them woods below. And way off is them long rows of spurs reachin' to the Yadkin Valley. Of an evening after sunset you can see'm sort of mist over and edge into the night.

"When the first stars commence a-shining it's mostly all deep and quiet like. Except way over east across the Yadkin they's just a rim of purple layin' over the Brushy Mountains."

Calloway Gap
265.2 miles
elev. 3,439

Elijah Calloway, a Scotch-Irishman from Tennessee, settled on this Blue Ridge site before the Civil War when "there wasn't a stick of timber cut on the land." Since that day the forests have disappeared over the rugged land swells, replaced by tilled fields and pastures. Only the steep valleys and rocky mountaintops remain covered with trees. Four generations of Calloways farmed the old homestead before they finally sold out and moved away.

Mt. Jefferson Overlook
266.9 miles
elev. 3,699

Mt. Jefferson, honoring one of our revered founding fathers, was so designated in 1952. A state park is located along the 4,515 foot summit.

The mountain hulks over the town of Jefferson. In late afternoon the sun disappears behind the mountain, resulting in a dark appearance in contrast to other high points still bright in the sun.

This may explain the previous name of Negro Mountain that dates into the 1700s. J.P. Arthur, the historian, relates a more colorful origin. In his history of western North Carolina, he states that the mountain was named for a runaway slave recaptured there during the Revolution.

Slaves on the getaway hid out on the mountain while traveling north during the troubled times building up to the Civil War. Several of the native white families, opposed to slavery, aided the fugitives with food and guidance.

Accordingly, the mountain became known as a way-station on the "underground railway." The mountain's commanding height and location above the town of Jefferson at a junction of highways made it a logical temporary hideout for runaway slaves. But any notion of highly organized activity by secret agents operating on the mountain is not in accord with known facts. The underground railroad of pre-Civil War days was largely an unorganized flight of slaves, drifting northward singly or in groups. The majority relied mainly on the North Star. A small percentage of slaves were spirited northward by anti-slavery groups, but most "passengers" were on their own.

"It's a place where a man can go and rescue hisself." So states Will Reeves (1956), the gray-haired son of a slave who lived in the shadow of the mountain.

View of Betsy's Rock
267.8 miles
elev. 3,400

black locust	*pignut*
red maple	*flowering*
red oak	*dogwood*
white oak	*rosebay*
scarlet oak	*rhododendron*

On the front left the steep, forested slope is cut by a narrow slash of gray rock. A small waterfall whispers and writhes its way to the bottom. A short distance below the top of the falls is a moss-covered ledge known as Betsy's Rock. "Aunt Betsy Pierce lived there in the time of The War (Civil War, of course) with two children. One died. She made her living gathering up all kinds of herbs and digging fur sang (ginseng). She carried them to Arthur Cowles' store 9 miles yonder way on Gap Creek." *(Uncle Newt)*

Benge Gap
268 miles
elev. 3,296

The location of a wagon-road crossing over the Blue Ridge, and of a former post office, Benge, N.C. "Hit took the name after my grandfather on account of he owned all the land for a long ways around." *(Will Benge, 1956)*

Phillips Gap
269.8 miles
elev. 3,221

When the people for whom the mountain features are named came and settled this country, it was very much in vogue to raise large families. But to have them all live was another matter. Doctors were few and far between.

Caleb Phillips and his wife, the durable "Mei-me Brown," raised every one of their 24 children. This brings to mind the tragic story of Aunt Orelena Puckett of Virginia, who likewise had 24 children, but lost them all.

DOGTROT CABIN

The numerous Phillipses, several of them twins, grew up in a "dogtrot" cabin right where the motor road now passes. A dogtrot is actually two cabins connected by a porchlike "breezeway," or "dogtrot." Probably Caleb started out with one unit and then had to add another.

Descendants of Caleb and "Mei-me" say that when the whole family was home they could "hoe a common field of corn" by the time their mother made breakfast.

Lewis Fork
270.2 miles
elev. 3,290

The south prong of the Lewis Fork heads below the overlook, gathering water from seeps and springs. It flows over the tiny plateau in the foreground and glides to the Yadkin.

Near the confluence of Lewis Fork and the Yadkin, about 15 green and rambling miles below, a family or two built their homes on a knoll many years ago. The main road between Boone and Wilkesboro passed by, and the community, known as Lewis Fork, held promise of growing into a permanent place on the map. But progress came and rerouted the highway between the main towns. No one hears of Lewis Fork today.

A mile or two from Lewis Fork, on the Yadkin at Holman's Ford, there once lived a young hunter. He loved life in the wilderness. When new settlers moved in, he headed into the still unopened West. He kept on leading the way. Everyone knows about Daniel Boone.

E. B. Jeffress Park
271.9 miles
600 acres

Rest rooms; drinking fountain; picnic tables; Cascades Nature Trail.

North Carolina honors a native son in the land where his

pride lies fulfilled and content. In 1934, as chairman of the state highway commission, he worked tirelessly and effectively to persuade the federal government to situate the Blue Ridge Parkway on its present location.

Cascades Nature Trail

A nature trail leads from the parking area to the cascades. Signs describe plants and wildlife along the way. The forest is chiefly oak and hickory. Beneath the trees is still another forest of rhododendron and mountain laurel, jungle-thick and evergreen.

DOGHOBBLE OR DROOPING LEUCOTHOE

The trail dips into a cove with new trees and atmosphere; Fraser magnolia, hemlock, and birch. Falls Creek runs alongside, deceptively lazy. Abruptly it cascades down a slick spillway. Spray leaps like glints of quicksilver. Rollicking, foam-lipped eddies slide down and out of sight, showing briefly again twisting around a big rock. 'Way below, the sunlit valley gleams through a keyhole arbor of trees.

Cool Spring Baptist Church Jesse Brown Cabin
272.6 miles

Squire Phillips, a relative of the prolific Caleb of Phillips Gap, recalled attending a funeral at the church in his boyhood, "during the year of the surrender." The church had a rib-pole roof, a form of construction resorted to when nails were scarce. The rows of shingle-like "roof-boards," or "shakes" were sandwiched between several pairs of poles extending rib-like along each side of the peaked roof. Eventually, the church "melted down." Some of the timbers were salvaged to build a shed for horses and cattle.

The church probably never had a regular congregation. Most of "the preachin's" were outdoor affairs. Folks came from miles away to hear the soul-raising sermons of Willie Lee and Bill Church. "I guess they'd come two hundred miles or more and have their horses tied to ever bush. People split logs and laid'm acrost each other for seats." (Bill Day, Deep Gap, N.C. 1954)

The Jesse Brown cabin resides beneath a broad red maple that once sheltered preachers Willie Lee and Bill Church. Several families have lived in the cabin since it was built in the late 1800s. Jesse Brown, a tenant farmer, was one of the first to live on the land. Jesse tended sheep and cattle for Colonel Jim Horton, a prosperous country gentleman from Lenoir.

The upland meadows, then as now, were frequently fog-bound. "One time a friend met up with Jesse and asked what he'd been a-doin'. He tole he'd been a-feeling through the fog all day for Horton's cattle." *(John Church, Deep Gap, N.C., 1954)*

The cabin, distinctive for its sharply pitched roof, is soundly constructed, with sturdy, well-matched logs. The tenants in 1900 were satisfied with their cabin, but desired to live closer to a water supply. Rather than build a new dwelling, they moved their home, log by log, to its pre-

Jesse Brown Cabin and Cool Spring Baptist Church

sent site and reassembled it. Cool Spring, bubbling forth fresh and clear beneath its spring house, gave them a refreshing reward.

**Elk Mountain
Overlook
View of
Yadkin Valley**
*274.3 miles
elev. 3,795*

Roadside easel: Bloom Time Along the Parkway

The name Yadkin is one of the oldest in the region and originates from "Yeatkin," an Indian village once situated on the banks of the river.

In the summer of 1674 James Needham and Gabriel Arthur were sent from Virginia by Abraham Woods, the Indian trader, to negotiate an agreement with the Cherokee. Enroute, they camped at the Indian village and recorded its name in their journal.

The Indians were probably members of the Saura tribe, an ill-fated group of the Piedmont. By the time the white settlers appeared their race had all but vanished. The name is believed to mean "big tree," or "place of the big trees."

The cleared area below the overlook is an old landmark known as the Fire Scald. Like Coiner's Dead 'nin' in Virginia, mile 6, no evidence for its name remains. The trees supposedly girdled and deadened by Mr. Coiner have long since moldered away. So has the "scalded" appearance of the mountain slopes.

RED FOX

The Scald, like other similar "listening posts" along the Parkway, once served as a rendezvous for generations of fox hunters. Their opinion of the sport was not shared by their women folk. "O, law! That was the awfulest place for fox hunters ever been. They run them hounds all day and all night." *(Zora Powell Woodie, 1954)*

Deep Gap
*276.4 miles
elev. 3,142*

U.S. 421: Boone, 11 miles west; Wilkesboro, 26 miles east.

In the final days of the Civil War, Union raiders probed into the backwaters of the South. Along their line of march, they occupied Deep Gap and dug in.

"In compliance with instructions from Major General Stoneman...on the sixth instant I proceeded from Taylorsville, Tennessee, to Boone, North Carolina, meeting Colonel Kirk, who left this camp on the 5th instant with the 2d and 3d North Carolina mountain infantry. On the morning of the 7th, the 2d North Carolina infantry, Major Bahney commanding, occupied Deep Gap...At all points mentioned I examined the ground, located and gave particular instructions for building rough but formidable fieldworks." *(Report of Brig. Gen. David Tilstan, Fourth Division Commander)*

General Stoneman's men came from Tennessee and raided the mountain and Piedmont towns of North Carolina and Virginia. A unit under his command bivouackd at Deep Gap and put up earthworks to protect the flanks. Numerous skirmishes were fought against the various home guards between March 28 and April

23, but the conclusive action had been settled at Appomattox on April 9 with Lee's surrender to Grant.

View from Carroll Gap
278.3 miles
elev. 3,430

Preacher Sid Carroll lived in the gap most of his life with his wife and family. He preached at several local places of worship including the Mount Perion church in the valley below. Husband and wife are buried side by side in a lonesome graveyard, a mile south, high in a saddle between two knobs:

Sidney T. Carroll 1845-1914   Nancy Carroll 1850-1920

Access to U.S. 221 and U.S. 421
280.8 miles
elev. 3,333
Boone, 7 miles west

The flourishing town of Boone, N.C., originated at the site of Jordon Councill's store. An early date of record is the establishment of a post office in 1823. Mr. Councill's trading center became known as Boone Post Office in 1850 and was incorporated under its present name in 1871.

The development and progress of Boone is closely associated with Appalachian State University, one of the leading institutions in the State. Two determined brothers, B.B. and D.D. Dougherty, established the Watauga Academy, a private three-teacher school, in 1899. In 1903 it became a state school and has matched strides with the thirst for education. Known as Appalachian State University since 1967, the school offers a four-year curriculum, with graduate studies.

Town and university dwell in a vitalizing mountain climate, and play host to thousands of summer residents and visitors. Many come to see "Horn in the West," a drama that carries you into those exciting times when the "horn of freedeom, blowing in the West," beckoned to the venturesome and brave.

Each December, Boone holds a busy and colorful burley tobacco auction. Farmers from Watauga and adjoining counties bring their sun-cured leaves to the warehouse and the nimble chant of the auctioneer.

One pleasant day in August, not long ago, an old resident looked about and said, "This place sure has changed. It used to the muddiest place ever was. They didn't have no paved streets nor nothin'. I remember one time this chicken tried to cross the road. The further it got the more trouble it had pullin' one leg after the other. Finally, it got mired up out there in the middle and couldn't move one way or the other."

Grandview
281.7 miles
elev. 3,240

In 1933 a local businessman, Grant Green, built the Mountain View store nearby to serve the travelers on U.S. Rt. 421. He enjoyed the same superlative view seen from the overlook. One day, after Mr. Green had been in business a year or so, a man from West Virginia stopped by. He gazed admiringly at the scenery. "A grand view." Mr. Green agreed and renamed his place accordingly.

The narrow valley, in the foreground below, is drained by Boone's Camp Branch. Daniel had a home base, 1751-69, at the foot of the Blue Ridge on the upper Yadkin River. He went on many long hunts into the mountains. When night came he camped where water and shelter were most convenient. The name of the branch implies that "Dan'l" frequently hunted and made camp hereabouts.

Boones' Trace Overlook
285.1 miles
elev. 3,270

Daniel Boone, 1734-1820, moved from Pennsylvania as a young man with his parents and other family members, and settled in the Carolina Piedmont (1751). He was a restless, adventurous man, not suited to the life of a "scratch" farmer nurturing his land. He made many hunting trips into the mountains, extending as far as Tennessee and Kentucky. Sometimes he went with a companion or two, sometimes alone. He learned much from the Indians. They were often foes, but with mutual respect and understanding.

A frequent route from his various Yadkin Valley homesites crossed what is now the Parkway and led into the mountains and the unknown.

In more settled times he would have been a debt-ridden dreamer who lived to roam and hunt; who thought of his wife and children lovingly, but often at a great distance.

But he became the superb woodsman and Indian fighter, cool in a crisis, who led settlers west through Cumberland Gap into the Blue Grass. Boone learned his skills in North Carolina and proved them in Kentucky. He was the man of the hour, time and time again.

Bamboo
285.5 miles
elev. 2,362

During the time this community selected a name for its newly created post office, large stands of white pine were sripped of their bark before the trees were felled. Someone, according to a still prevailing practice, bought the "bark rights." The dried inner bark was sold for use in preparing cough medicines.

Generally the bark is stripped from the saw-logs, but in this instance it was apparently removed from the standing timber. And so there stood the trees, naked and white, like bamboo.

RAVEN

Raven Rocks
289.5 miles
elev. 3,810

Ravens nest in rocky outcrops much like the one below the overlook. "Raven Rocks" is a familiar name in the highlands and few counties or even townships are without one.

The large black birds are still common along the Parkway, but are no longer seen through the farm country of the plateau. They find a good supply of raven rocks in the rugged forests north of Roanoke and south from the Black Mountains.

The long, high dome of Flat Top Mountain dominates the horizon across the Aho Valley. The white-painted Cone Manor House shows small yet vividly on its slopes.

Yadkin Valley
289.8 miles
elev. 3,840

WHITE PINE

Between the descending spurs sloping from the Blue Ridge flows the fluid network of the Yadkin headwaters. It forms from springs and seeps filtering into the hollows. The newborn trickles have no course of their own but follow the whim of the terrain. Their way is hindered by dead branches and deflected by leaves. Many of the moist pathways die in dry weather.

Thin, straight streams gather the water and feed into the narrow valleys between the spurs. They become more forceful and cut into the earth and define themselves with banks and a stream bed. Each is now important enough to have a name: Blackberry Branch, Groundhog Branch, Horse Branch, and Martin Branch.

At the foot of the nearby hills they merge. The new stream flows toward a great valley between the Blue Ridge and the distant Brushy Mountains. En route it collects the waters of Baily Camp Creek where loggers used to fell the big yellow poplar and white pine. At the foothills community of Richmond it collects the waters of Dennis Creek.

In appearance this stream is like thousands of others draining the border of the Blue Ridge. But it is the headwaters of the Yadkin, the river destined to collect the dashing mountain water from Blowing Rock north to Virginia and carry it leisurely toward the sea.

Thunder Hill
290.4 miles
elev. 3,800

When storms darken the skies, the blackest, biggest thunderheads gather over Thunder Hill. They seethe with electric rumblings that build into rapid-fire crescendos and boom in the wake of lightning.

The view from Thunder Hill looks into Blackberry Valley below. During intensive logging in the years during and after World War I, the trees were harvested and the second growth provided good forage for cattle. In such openings the blackberry is quickly established. For years folks trouped to Blackberry Valley each June and July to pick the juicy fruit. Now most of the bushes have been grubbed out to make way for pasture.

U.S. 221 and
U.S. 321
291.9 miles

North 9 miles to Boone: Blowing Rock, 2 miles south on U.S. 221; Lenoir, 21 miles southeast on U.S. 321.

A Note about the Author:
Park Ranger and Naturalist, 1948–55

Bill Lord came to the Blue Ridge Parkway in 1948, a recently discharged infantryman and a still more recent graduate in zoology from Michigan State University. He was pursuing an ambition engendered in his Huck Finn and Tom Sawyer years to become a naturalist in the National Park Service. The Parkway didn't fit his concept of a national park. No grizzly bears or buffalo. But this was his chance to get into the service and he took it.

He found himself park rangering forty miles of the "scenic," not on a horse, but in a Pontiac coupe. He dwelled, not in a rustic cabin, but in a quiet upstairs apartment in the unhurried county seat of Floyd, Virginia, respectfully referred to by the local gentry as Floyd Court House.

He still remembers one crisp and sun-bright February morn. He had not yet been assigned a vehicle nor traveled the full length of his patrol. His time was spent in the Rocky Knob District Office learning the outline of his duties. The previous days had been cloudy and hemmed in, but now the sky was clear and the mountains revealed themselves. Warden Guy Dillon came in from a patrol in his pick-up truck and gestured to Bill. "Come along with me." Guy was mostly quiet the mile or two until they reached an overlook on Rocky Knob. He grinned and pointed over the mountain edge. "Go have a look." Guy knew that Bill would be wondrous at the view, and no one was ever more right. He felt aloft and weightless — right by the precipice, absorbing the shadowed, shaggy length of Rock Castle Gorge below and the singing, sweeping far-beyond of foothills, farm, and forest. That's where the guidebook was born:

> To tell the story
> True to the people and the land
> This main regard
> And be a chronicler
> A minstrel
> A worthy bard